WHY GOOD KIDS ACT CRUEL

The Hidden Truth about the Pre-Teen Years

CARL PICKHARDT, PhD

 sourcebooks

155,4248
PIC

Published by Sourcebooks, Inc.
P.O. Box 4410, Naperville, Illinois 60567-4410
(630) 961-3900
Fax: (630) 961-2168
www.sourcebooks.com

Library of Congress Cataloging-in-Publication Data

Pickhardt, Carl E.
   Why good kids act cruel: the hidden truth about the pre-teen years / Carl Pickhardt.
      p. cm.
   Includes bibliographical references and index.
   1. Aggressiveness in adolescence. 2. Aggressiveness in youth. 3. Bullying. 4. Bullying in schools. I. Title.
   BF724.3.A34P53 2009
   155.42'48--dc22

2009036477

Printed and bound in the United States of America.
VP 10 9 8 7 6 5 4 3 2 1

To all those young people who brave the social cruelties of their middle school years and come out stronger for it.

Disclaimer:

Unless otherwise attributed, all quotations cited and case examples used are fictional, created to reflect concerns and to illustrate situations similar in kind but not in actuality to those I have heard from clients over the years.

THE PROBLEM

"Every school year, literally millions of teenagers suffer from emotional violence in the form of bullying, harassment, stalking, intimidation, humiliation, and fear."

Garbarino, James and Ellen deLara, And Words Can Hurt Forever: How to Protect Adolescents from Bullying, Harassment, and Emotional Violence *(New York: Free Press, 2003) viii.*

"Some years ago, in the candor of the exam room, a seventh-grade boy told me that he really didn't have friends at school and that he sometimes found himself being picked on. I gave him the pediatric line on bullying: It shouldn't be tolerated, and there are things schools can do about it. Let's talk to your parents, let's have your parents talk to the school; adult interventions can change the equation. And he was horrified. He shook his head vehemently and asked me please not to interfere, and above all, not to say a word to his mother, who was out in the waiting room because I had asked her to give us some privacy. He wouldn't have told me this at all, he said, except he thought our conversation was *private*. The situation at school wasn't all that bad; he could handle it. He wasn't in any danger, wasn't getting hurt; he was just a little lonely. His parents, he said, thought he was fine, that he had lots of friends, and he wanted to keep it that way."

Klaas, Perri, MD, "What to Do When Patient Says, 'Please Don't Tell Mom,'" (New York Times, December 9, 2008) D1.

"The school is without doubt where most of the bullying occurs."

Olweus, Dan, Bullying at School *(Malden, MA: Blackwell Publishing, 1993)* 21.

"Your child has a right to be educated in an environment that is free of fear and harassment."

Coloroso, Barbara, The Bully, the Bullied, and the Bystander *(New York: HarperCollins, 2003)* 193.

"Educational leaders and teachers have the unique role of making personal connections and shaping young students' attitudes beyond the academic scope of the classroom. This role places them *in loco parentis,* a position that requires them to do everything in their power to prevent violent incidences on campus just as if they were the child's parents protecting them from violence outside of school."

Schoonover, Brian, Zero Tolerance Discipline Policies *(Bloomington, IN: iUniverse, 2009)* 55.

"Driven by newly documented slumps in learning, by crime rates, and by high dropout rates in high school, educators... across the nation are struggling to rethink middle school and how best to teach adolescents at a transitional juncture of self-discovery and hormonal change...Middle school teachers...must guide these students through the profound transformations of adolescence."

Gootman, Elissa, "Trying to Find Solutions in Chaotic Middle Schools," (New York Times, January 3, 2007) A1.

CONTENTS

CHAPTER ONE

SOCIAL CRUELTY

Walking down the crowded hall between classes the first day of middle school, Ellen unintentionally bumped another girl into a locker. Turning to apologize, Ellen saw the girl already talking to a couple friends. One of them angrily glared at her and said, "Why don't you watch where you're going, Hula Hips?" Then the other friend took up the call, "Watch out for Hula Hips!" And so, at the beginning of the year, a painful nickname was born from that casual encounter. By the end of the week, the name had stuck with repetition, picked up by other students, including a few she had known in elementary school and even some boys who thought it was funny to single her out for ridicule. "Watch out for Hula Hips!" they laughed. But it was not so funny for Ellen. The meanness of the teasing hurt. Welcome to middle school!

Why do many good children increasingly treat each other badly starting as early as late elementary school; *when* does this meanness become most common; *what* are the objectives of this deliberate mistreatment; *how* is it typically delivered; and *what* can parents and teachers do to help children in response? These are the basic questions that I try to answer in this book, which is intended to be both descriptive and prescriptive—proposing how adult understanding and intervention can help stem the harm.

My term for this intentional meanness is *social cruelty*—aggressively attacking another child with words or actions directed to injure the victim's well-being, to damage his or her standing, or to simply assert the aggressor's dominance.

I believe:

- *Why* it occurs is rooted in early adolescence (roughly beginning around ages nine to thirteen) when the *insecurity* and *vulnerability* of separating from childhood is coupled with the desire for increased *social independence* to act more grown-up.

- *When* it is most problematic is during the middle school years, because almost all the students have been destabilized and challenged by early adolescent change by then.

- *What* motivates this behavior is the need to protect diminished self-worth by derogating the worth of others, to attack others to preempt getting hurt first, to defend after being attacked, to give payback for injury received, to assert dominance, and to claim or hold one's social place.

- *How* it is typically acted out includes tactics of *teasing, exclusion, bullying, rumoring* (spreading rumors), and *ganging up.*

- *What* parents and teachers can do is become knowledgeable about the changing world of children at this vulnerable age, coach them in how to cope with social cruelty, help them develop a constructive code for treating each other, and get involved when significant acts of social cruelty occur.

The first step for adults is to understand how the potentiality of social cruelty in the lives of late elementary and middle school students is rooted in the dislocation, insecurity, and need for more social independence that comes with early adolescent change. The second step for adults is to stay sufficiently informed about the young person's increasingly independent social world so they can monitor and influence how early adolescents treat each other. The more youth groups are abandoned by significant adults (parents and teachers), the more social cruelty is likely to flourish due to the rigorous rules of social survival at this vulnerable age.

In addition, when adults ignore acts of social cruelty, they become complicit with the problem. The victim gets no support. The community of peers becomes more unsafe. And the victimizer learns to become more aggressive, more antisocial, and intentionally harmful while he or she grows. Such development can set the stage for psychological and social adjustment problems later in life. This is another reason why adults must not leave early adolescents entirely alone to determine social conduct amongst themselves.

Staying informed, however, is not easy for adults, because young people's new sense of social independence works against involvement. Adolescents want to have a social world apart from adults, one that is private about what happens, and that includes incidents of social cruelty. In addition to young people's need for privacy, their pride in keeping up appearances, and their desire to keep adults out, there is also the "don't-tell-on-peers" code of the school yard that encourages secrecy and silence.

In fact, social cruelty is protected by this conspiracy of silence. Most acts of social cruelty go undetected by adults because they are unreported. Young people don't tell you, because to let adults know of these incidents, they would have to sacrifice some social independence and risk serious social payback. To quote what one middle school student told me: "Snitches get stitches."

So when a teacher asks the kids what happened out in the hall, they pretend they don't know. After all, it's safer to lie to a teacher than to tell on a peer, because reprisal from the other students can always come their way.

Besides, most teachers don't know what is going on. Asked about their last class, most middle school teachers will likely remember how students responded to instructions and either complied with or resisted their need for order. Ask students what happened in the same class, and they will describe another level of social interaction that teachers can miss. Teachers don't hear what the students whisper; they don't see the looks that are given; and they don't read the notes that are passed. They don't know the threats that are made, and they don't hear the harsh words that are said or the names that are called. They don't sense the jealousies; they don't notice the rivalries developing; and they aren't told the stories that are being spread around school. They don't witness the bumps and pokes that are delivered (until they explode into a fight). They don't pick up on who is not talking to whom today or who is fixing whom with a hostile glare. But it is in this second world, which is mostly hidden from adults, where social cruelty occurs.

As for parents, they may not know, because their child doesn't want them to know how he or she is fearful or friendless, or perhaps feels threatened or alone. Typically, if young people are on the receiving end of social cruelty, they will make this difficult situation even worse by blaming themselves for not fitting in, insufficient popularity, or inadequate toughness. In turn, young people end up blaming parents for their ignorance of the situation. The primary reasons young people cite for not disclosing the social cruelty they receive at school is that 1) they believe parents wouldn't believe that kind of thing goes on; 2) it might imply that something is wrong with them; or 3) adults will intervene in ways that will only make things worse.

To paraphrase one student's complaint: "My parents just don't get it! But if I told them, they'd think something's wrong with me. They haven't a clue what seventh grade is really like. They don't know what I face each day! My report card—that's all they care about. That's the least of my problems!" Actually, the child is mistaken. There's much more breadth of caring in his parents than he gives them credit for. His early adolescent determination to manage his own life at school causes him to keep them in ignorance of the harsh realities that can come with managing this independent social world.

■ ■ ■

My primary motivation for writing this book is to help parents "get it." If you learn about social cruelty and show you know what can go on in your adolescent child's social life, your beleaguered son or daughter will be much more likely to tell you what (if any) mistreatment is actually going on.

So, specifically what are the social cruelties that come to the forefront during the middle school years? Five categories of meanness repeatedly emerged in my discussions while counseling young people:

- *Teasing*

- *Exclusion*

- *Bullying*

- *Rumoring*

- *Ganging up*

Now, consider these categories in more detail to get a better sense of each.

Teasing

A child can be a victim of *teasing* when given an insulting nickname, when put down for appearance or performance, when ridiculed for standing out or not fitting in, or when laughed at for what he or she says or doesn't know. *Teasing is the act of making fun of a difference in someone to criticize his or her traits, diminish his or her social standing, and set him or her apart socially.* The cruel message is "There's something wrong with you." Teasing is intended to humiliate with insults.

Exclusion

A child can be a victim of *exclusion* when students ignore him or her in class, deny him or her a place at the lunch table, see that he or she is not included in gatherings outside of school, shun classroom contact so that he or she feels isolated, or expel him or her from membership in their group. *Exclusion is the act of refusing to let someone associate with others or join a group.* The cruel message is "You don't belong." Exclusion is intended to isolate with rejection.

Bullying

A child can be a victim of *bullying* when possessions are stolen or vandalized, when threats are made "to get you after school" in person or over the phone, when he or she is verbally attacked over the Internet, or when the child is routinely hit or shoved or beaten up. *Bullying is the act of verbally or physically intimidating, injuring, coercing, or dominating another person.* The cruel message is "You can be pushed around." Bullying is intended to frighten with threatened or actual harm.

Rumoring

A child can be a victim of *rumors* when others circulate salacious notes, make up and tell malicious stories (in person, over the phone, or via the Internet) about a person to create a false impression he or she will have trouble living down, or reveal and distort a secret trustingly told in confidence. *Rumoring is the act of using gossip to spread lies or secrets about another person that demeans his or her social reputation.* The cruel message is "You can't control the bad things that people say about you that others are ready to believe." Rumoring is intended to slander with confidential truths or blatant lies.

Ganging Up

A child can be a victim of being *ganged up on* when no one is on his or her side or when multiple students verbally or physically use any of the other four kinds of social cruelty to attack a single person. It creates a sense of solidarity between the attackers and extreme vulnerability in the object of their attack. *Ganging up is the act of the many using their greater numbers to torment one particular person.* The cruel message is "You have no friends to support you, only enemies against you." Ganging up is intended to pit the group against the individual.

Of course, these five forms of social cruelty often overlap. At worst, they can all combine to extremely cruel effect—when someone is teased, bullied, rumored, ganged up on, and then excluded from the group. Those on the receiving end of such an onslaught truly feel that everyone has turned against them: *I don't have any friends!* these victims think. *Everybody hates me!*

Each kind of social cruelty preys on a different early adolescent fear:

- Teasing preys on the *fear of being inferior*: "Something is wrong with me." It undermines self-esteem.

- Exclusion preys on the *fear of isolation*: "I have no friends." It accentuates loneliness.

- Bullying preys on the *fear of weakness*: "I'm unable to stand up for myself." It increases a sense of impotence.

- Rumor preys on the *fear of defamation*: "People say mean things about me." It slurs reputation.

- Ganging up preys on the *fear of persecution*: "Everyone has
  turned against me." It makes one feel like a social outcast.

It's important for parents to understand that this is not a
simple matter of "bad" kids treating each other badly. Rather,
it is about good kids doing something they know is mean to
survive a psychologically insecure time, within a more independent and uncertain social world. Social cruelty is antisocial
behavior that serves a social purpose. It is intentionally hurtful
behavior that young people engage in because there is something of social value to be gained—to assert dominance or
protect against attack or to establish standing, for example. As
discussed in the next chapter about early adolescent change, I
believe the potential for social cruelty is rooted in the child's
development at this complicated age.

■ ■ ■

Though certainly aggressive, most acts of social cruelty are
primarily compensatory, retaliatory, or preemptive in nature, attacking the vulnerabilities and insecurities of others to deny,
safeguard, or divert the focus from the aggressor's own insecurities. Young people tease about what they don't want to be
teased about. They spread rumors to create lies they don't want
told about themselves. They bully others partly to prevent being
pushed around. They exclude others to protect their own inclusion. They gang up on someone to make him or her the victim

so they don't have to occupy that dreaded role. To help your child during this time, it will be important to understand this, as well as the other nuances of social cruelty.

First, there is some degree of difference in how boys and girls engage in social cruelty. From what I have seen, boys do somewhat more of the bullying and teasing, while girls do somewhat more of the exclusion and rumoring; however, both seem to do about the same amount of ganging up—though boys are more prone to enact it physically, and girls are more to prone to do it socially.

Because of how male and female children are still socialized growing up (boys are more competitive and performance-focused, and girls are more confiding and relationship-focused), there tends to be some degree of difference in how they engage in social cruelty. Boys often take more latitude for the direct expression of anger and aggression than girls, who often elect to be more indirect—hence the reputation of girls being more sneaky and manipulative than boys when it comes to social cruelty. Boys are often more "in-your-face" aggressive; girls are often "behind-your-back" aggressive. Both are equally aggressive, just in different ways. Girls are expected to mask their aggression more. As one teacher described it to me: "Girls are just 'nicer' about being mean. They can do the insincere smile. Few boys are good at that."

All five kinds of social cruelty are expressions of social aggression through which the perpetrator or perpetrators seek some kind of benefit—usually higher standing, more power, better association, or confirmed control. Sometimes, adults, teachers, and even parents will hold the victim responsible either for bringing it on or for not fighting it off. This is a mistake. When adults blame the victim for social cruelty, two kinds of damage are done. First, the victim is encouraged to blame him or herself—hence, statements such as "I deserved it," "I brought it on myself," "They're right to treat me this way," and "I'm just no good!" Secondly, the perpetrator is cleared of responsibility for the social aggression that he or she committed—hence statements such as "I was just having fun," "She brought it on herself," "She's making a big deal over nothing," and "I didn't do anything wrong." When parents or teachers ignore or condone this behavior, they only encourage its continuation.

Parents sometimes discount social cruelty when their child is acting as a participant, denying the truth of what happened to defend their son or daughter, or even themselves. "Our daughter wouldn't act that way. We don't believe it. We've taught her better." Teachers can condone social cruelty when they believe confronting it will likely create more classroom trouble. "We just need to let the incident go, put it behind us, and move on." Both groups of adults are shirking their responsibility to become involved.

In social cruelty, frequency of occurrence makes an enormous difference. Once started, it is more likely to happen again in the future. And when incidents are repeated, the magnitude of the harm inflicted is vastly increased. Thus, when teasing routinely leads to attaching a hate name to someone, when systematic exclusion leads to shunning a person, when relentless bullying becomes stalking, when widespread rumoring destroys someone's reputation, and when constant ganging up creates ongoing persecution, then social cruelty can have devastating effects. For instance, ganging up can become a morning recreation for some eighth graders on the bus who start their day wondering who can get that little sixth grader with glasses to cry. In this case, "fun" for the many is agony for the one.

Social cruelty can also shape future conduct in both victim and perpetrator alike. Adolescents are tomorrow's adults, so as today's adults (parents and teachers), we need to train them to treat each other safely and respectfully while we still can. When allowed to continue, social cruelty can influence the formation of both the victim and the perpetrator, because present experience shapes future behavior. A victim of teasing can become more guarded; the person teasing can become more sarcastic. A victim of exclusion can become less socially confident; the person excluding can become more socially manipulative. A victim of bullying can become more anxious; the bully can become more coercive. A victim of rumoring can become more distrustful; the person rumoring can become more inclined to spread lies. A victim of ganging up can become more easily overwhelmed in social situations; a person participating in ganging up can become more easily swayed by peer pressure.

At worst, victims who take ongoing mistreatment to heart can be at risk of serious psychological harm. In the extreme, protracted torment at the hands of peers can drive victims into emotional devastation that is concealed from even those who know them best. Then, young people who have had "enough" can bring violence to school to act out unsuspected shame and rage, or they may bring their self-loathing home and act destructively after school against themselves. These acts of revenge punish the hostile world or attempt to put an end to personal suffering. Thankfully, such drastic incidents are the exception and not the rule, but they inform the adult world about how these students' acts of desperation can follow wherever social cruelty reigns. For persistent victims, social cruelty is angering, depressing, demeaning, frightening, humiliating, isolating, hurtful, and shameful. *Significant social cruelty has serious emotional consequences.*

■ ■ ■

Then, of course, there is the immediate academic cost. If a young person is constantly anxious about the classroom, the hallway, the lunchroom, and the playground cruelty they suffer at the hands of peers, or the mistreatment on the bus to and from school, concerns for social safety are going to take precedence over his or her motivation for classroom learning. *Because social cruelty undermines the victim's social safety, it often reduces academic focus and school performance.*

More importantly, the cost of social cruelty is not limited to the student harmed. Everyone knows that what happens to one can happen to all. It only takes witnessing one dramatic incident of social cruelty for bystanders to start worrying: "What if that happens to me?" And now they invest emotional energy in being on guard, being watchful, being careful, and being afraid as they cope with their school day. It's not that students don't learn to deal with this lack of safety—they do—but the price of this adjustment is precious energy and attention diverted from learning, not to mention the toll it takes on their peace of mind.

Every act of social cruelty not only endangers the victim, but puts everyone on guard by undermining the social safety of all; each act is an example of what can happen to anyone who is not careful. This is why everyone is victimized. As one twelve-year-old told his friend who was pushed around by some older kids on the school bus: "What they did to you they could do to me." Perhaps the cruelest part of social cruelty, especially for those on the receiving end, is seeing how friends are indirectly impacted and how they will not stand up for you. It is the same principle of domestic abuse. Any violence against one member of the family by another threatens the safety of all.

Thus, schools must do more to face this issue head-on. Some believe addressing students about social cruelty is a waste of instructional time, because this investment of attention is at the expense of academic learning. However, I say that academic learning will suffer if schools do not address these issues. I believe the most academically successful schools, particularly during the middle school years, are those in which students feel emotionally and physically safe, where there are no daily worries about getting hurt, and where it is not necessary to take precautions to protect oneself from possible harm. During the middle school years, a time when performance drops for so many students who are derailed by the demands of adolescent change, schools must act to limit the incidents of social cruelty and the distracting sense of jeopardy they can in turn create.

■ ■ ■

By focusing on the early adolescent middle school years, I am not saying that younger children do not sometimes deliberately hurt each other. Of course they do. Left unsupervised on the playground, young children will use varieties of social cruelty to determine the social pecking order of dominance, exercising power in crudely brutal ways, such as saying, "The reason you can't play with us is because nobody likes you!" Nor am I saying that social cruelty cannot occur in high school; it can and does. By then, however, it is no longer driven by developmental insecurity but has become culturally endorsed behavior of a more serious kind, behavior that can ultimately lead to harassment, hate naming, sexual molestation, physical assaults, and intergroup violence. Now there is danger of real physical harm. All the more reasons for parents and teachers to educate, monitor, and intervene in the middle school years in an effort to instruct students in the humane social treatment of one another as they create constructive rules of conduct within their independent community of peers.

This window of opportunity for adults to influence an early adolescent's social behavior usually closes by the end of middle school when young people have formed enough sense of personal identity and claimed enough social security that they are now more comfortably set in their adolescent ways. By high school, the norms and habits of interpersonal conduct between peers have become socially established. It is in late elementary school and particularly middle school when parents and teachers have an opportunity to impact those norms of social treatment that young people develop with each other. These salient adults will never have such an opportunity for social influence again.

So the caution is simply this: If adults allow social cruelty to go uncorrected during the middle school years, worse damage will likely follow in high school.

■ ■ ■

In considering the five types of social cruelty—teasing, exclusion, bullying, rumoring, ganging up—I take a somewhat different approach from other writers on this topic. (For some excellent books on the subject, see my list in the Recommended Reading section.) I believe these acts of social cruelty are *symptoms* of an underlying emotional discomfort that largely originates in a common *cause*: the social dislocation and developmental insecurity of early adolescent change. In this sense, I follow a "medical" model in this book. I believe parents and school staff are best advised not only to address the symptoms but also to treat the cause.

Therefore, to give you an adequate understanding of each aspect of social cruelty and how to address each with your child, I take the following approach in this book. Chapter Two describes the *cause*, namely how early adolescent change begins to separate the young person from the old definition of child and relationship to family, creating developmental insecurity, personal vulnerability, and the need for social independence in the company of peers. I suggest strategies that parents can use at this critical juncture to stay connected with their son or daughter and retain beneficial influence as adolescence starts causing parent and child to grow apart.

Chapters Three through Seven each describe one of five kinds of social cruelty that are *symptoms* of the underlying cause. Each kind of social cruelty is explained in terms of its own psychological dynamics, and, within each chapter, I suggest how parents can help reduce the harm whether the child is the receiver or giver of mistreatment.

Chapter Eight describes *what the school can do* instructionally (the teacher), supportively (the counselor), and administratively (the principal), in collaboration with parents, to prevent, address, and decrease social cruelty among students. In conjunction with parents, these adults can do much to encourage students to create a school community in which it feels safe to learn.

As I have stated, early adolescence creates a window for adult influence during the middle school years (which closes come high school) that allows parents and teachers to help young people learn how to treat each other well at this socially independent age. Essentially, this book describes what social cruelty is, how it works, why it occurs, the damage it can do, and the various ways parents and school staff can stop some of the harm.

Adolescence is a challenging period of growth. It is a process of gathering power—from dependence at the beginning to independence at the end. The job of adults, at home and at school, is to help young people gather this power in appropriate ways. Social cruelty (teasing, exclusion, bullying, rumoring, ganging up) is an *in*appropriate way to gather personal and interpersonal power in the exercise of social independence. Adults need to help young people find better ways to relate to each other. *When it comes to moderating social cruelty,* *there is no substitute for adult awareness, involvement, and intervention in the early adolescent world.*

Hopefully, this book will help parents and school personnel in both public- and private-school settings better understand the problem and decide how to address it.

CHAPTER TWO

EARLY ADOLESCENCE

Coming back into the locker room from physical education, Reese was glad that embarrassment was over.
Physical education was his least favorite class, because it
showed him (and everybody else) how the bodies of other
boys were growing faster than his was, and he felt inferior in
comparison. Then he saw a couple of the bigger boys look at
him, whisper, and nod their heads as he got undressed. Just
after he had pulled off his shorts and was about to pull on
his pants, they rushed him, grabbed his pants, and left the
locker room laughing, leaving him with no pants to wear. To
the bigger boys, it was a funny joke, and it served as a message
about who was socially in charge. To Reese, the incident was
intimidating and humiliating, and it left him in a painful pre-
dicament. Elementary school had felt a lot safer than this.

Whenever I think of early adolescence and the middle
school years, I am reminded of Thomas Wolfe's extraordinary

title, *You Can't Go Home Again*. For me, this phrase captures the irredeemable loss and daunting challenge that besets young people when they realize that they must leave the confines of childhood, never to return to that simpler, sheltered, and supportive time. They can never "go home" again.

No longer a child and not yet an adult, they can only grow forward and begin the ten- to twelve-year adolescent struggle to finally become functionally independent. The beginning of adolescence can feel the hardest. Just as the middle school years lack the comfort and security of the elementary grades, early adolescence lacks the comfort and security of childhood.

Adolescence begins with loss, because the boy or girl can't start growing up without first letting go of what it was like to be defined and dealt with as a child. When the twelve-year-old girl protests about her father's traditional playfulness, she says, "Stop treating me like a child. I'm not your little girl anymore!" and she means it. But she misses the old connection she's lost, as evidenced by her anger when seeing dad cuddle with her two-year-old sister. "Stop doing that! Put her down! You'll spoil her!" she protests. And later she will engage in age-inappropriate teasing of the little sister to punish her for enjoying the affectionate treatment that the older sister misses but now feels too old to accept.

Growing up requires giving up, and the early adolescent experiences loneliness as a result of this loss. Part of that loss comes from forsaking some of the former childhood connections to family. He or she can no longer accept being "daddy's little girl" or "mommy's little boy." A second part of that loss comes from giving up the interests, enjoyments, and activities that mattered as a child. The adolescent doesn't want to do that "kid stuff" anymore, even though continuing scouts or swim team would still give him or her pleasure. This is why the young person is frustrated, bored, and restless. Boredom is a serious emotion at this age. It means he or she doesn't know what to do with him or herself, and it makes the adolescent easy prey for the impulsive ideas of peers, because doing anything feels better than doing nothing.

And then there is a third part of the loss. Early adolescents lose some of their contentment with being part of the family, fitting in, and enjoying parental company. The old mutual admiration society that brought about so much happiness in childhood more often becomes a mutual irritation society now that they are growing older. It feels very awkward. They know how they don't want to be defined and treated—as children. However, they don't yet know how they do want to be defined; they only know that they want to act older and become different. As for the parents, they too struggle with the loss.

Adolescence isn't just a process of change that happens to a child on the way to adulthood. It's a process that changes the young person's relationship with him or herself and with his or her parents. To the children, parents become harder to live with; to the parents, the children are harder to get along with. The relationship becomes more abrasive. Now, the young person becomes more resistant and argumentative with parents, who in turn become more impatient and critical with their child. Adolescence begins with a lot of loss: of the traditional childhood role, of the traditional childhood interests, and of the traditional childhood compatibility with parents.

For virtually all students, this journey of redefining themselves on older and as yet unspecified terms is underway by the middle school years. The child who looked to parents for guidance becomes the early adolescent who now discounts parental opinion and seeks that direction from peers. Hence, the early adolescent cares less about fitting into family and more about fitting in with friends. As the young person feels more disconnected from childhood and family, concern for acceptance from other students at school marks the new importance of belonging to a social world of peers.

The job of parents at this major transition point, namely when the child is pulling away and becoming more difficult to live with, is to stay connected with their son or daughter and keep that young person affiliated with family while adolescence is starting to grow them apart. When parents don't do this, and when the company of friends becomes "everything," then the potential for social cruelty increases, because now one's place in the world of peers starts to count for too much.

The developmental challenge for the early adolescent is huge. For some children, as early as the late elementary grades, they must begin to cast off the old childhood identity. They must begin redefining themselves, their relationship with their parents, their relationship with peers, and their roles in the larger, adult world. The developmental challenge for parents at this stage is to get up to speed on what specific changes to expect so they can deal with them effectively, and avoid overreacting in surprise, thus making an insecure transition worse. What follows is a playbook for understanding what kinds of early adolescent changes to expect from growing children.

Middle schoolers experience insecurity from three sources of change. First, there is *autonomy* and the determination to operate more on one's own terms. Second, there is *puberty* and the transformation to sexual maturity. And third, there is *social independence* and the creation of a family of peers. Let's start by detailing the insecurities created by autonomy.

Autonomy

At one of my workshops about adolescence for parents of sixth graders, two mothers were comparing notes.

"My son keeps telling me I don't understand," complained one.

"When you request information to better understand him," asked the other, "do you get it?"

"No!" the first mother replied in frustration.

"See," said the second, "that just proves it. He doesn't want you to know. He just wants to blame you for not understanding. He gets to feel more independent this way."

Autonomy occurs when your early adolescent is no longer content with being defined as your child, but instead shows signs that he or she wants to become more his or her own person. One of the most telling signs at this age is the desire, for example, for your daughter to redecorate her room, which is a reflection of self, or at least a reflection of the self that has caught her fascination, the one that she thinks is cool and older. A lot of "poster battles" arise at this age. Your son, for example is drawn to some countercultural or rebellious youth icons that may draw your fire: "No way am I going to allow that kind of image in our home!" There's just no self-respecting way he can afford to have teasing friends see him living in a little child's room when he is supposed to act more grown-up.

So parents need to think a minute. These images represent interests, not intentions. They are emblematic of the need for transformation; they are not statements about a specific transformation that will occur. Therefore, before you lower the boom of prohibition, you might want to ask your son or daughter to help you understand the popularity, the appeal of these popular figures. Understand that, and you will better understand your child's state of interest at this changing moment of time.

Now consider the enormous psychological change that this push for autonomy represents. Consider the three ways the child was previously anchored to the family and how the early adolescent pushes for more freedom of operation, definition, and association in order to shed his or her "child self."

The child (up to ages 8 to 10) was secured by three connections:

* *Attached* to parents for the love of their company and the safety they provided, the child was content with life within the family circle.

* *Compatible* with family values and established playmates, the child liked the comfort of familiar relationships and familiar surroundings.

* *Compliant* with parental demands and limits, the child liked pleasing them and consenting to do things their way.

Come early adolescence (beginning ages 9 to 13), these three primary connections, upon which so much stability depends, become more strained and even broken as the young person is no longer content being defined and treated like the child he or she was.

* *Separating* from family to explore more worldly experiences and to establish a distinct "family" of friends with whom he or she can belong, the early adolescent creates more

social distance from those at home. The goal of separation is more social independence.

- *Differentiating* oneself from the child he or she used to be, the early adolescent no longer fits in well with family and with some old friendships that do not accommodate new interests, values, and images he or she now finds appealing. The goal of differentiation is more individuality.

- *Opposing* family rules and restraints to establish more freedom of choice, the early adolescent's resistance and disagreement may provoke more conflict with parents than before. The goal of opposition is more self-determination.

Through separation, differentiation, and opposition, the boy or girl begins to cut the ties to childhood and allow adolescent growth to begin. This is the power of early adolescence: It *disconnects* the young person from childhood and creates an enormous sense of *insecurity* that is comprised of equal parts loneliness, uncertainty, and anxiety. The young person feels more alone and *lonely* from missing the old closeness and comfort with a parent and family that he or she has surrendered. Adolescents feel more confused and *uncertain* about how to manage growing up and chart a passage through an older world of experience, and they feel more worried and *anxious* about establishing social standing with their new community of acquaintances and friends. This is the *developmental insecurity* of early adolescence that no young person entirely escapes, and I believe this creates the *vulnerability* to giving and receiving social cruelty during the middle school years.

Now there are a host of hard trade-offs that young people must make, because growing up creates necessary losses that are painful to endure:

- To develop as adolescents, they have to reject their view of themselves as children.

- To become more self-determined, they must challenge parental authority.

- To experiment with becoming different, they must fit less into the family.

- To obtain new freedom, they must accept new risks and responsibilities.

- To assume new independence, they must let go of some old childhood dependencies.

- To form a family of friends, they must forsake some closeness with family at home.

- To make new friends, they may have to let some old friends go.

Because these trade-offs can be painful, they can cause the young person to send confusing double messages to parents, such as "let me do it, but do it for me," "leave me alone, but don't leave me out," "treat me older, but treat me younger."

Which way does the early adolescent want it? The answer is both ways, and that's okay. *This ambivalence is an insecure response to a liberating but uncomfortable change about which the young person feels honestly mixed.*

The beginning of this passage through adolescence is confounded by many contradictions that only add to the confusion:

- Adolescents who pull away from parents often feel abandoned by them, even though it is they who are pulling away.

- Adolescents who feel misunderstood by parents usually discount how they are keeping their parents in ignorance by communicating less.

- Adolescents who have become more confrontational for independence sake often feel it is their parents who have become harder to get along with.

- Adolescents who look larger in parental eyes and in the eyes of the world actually feel smaller and diminished in their own eyes, because now the world beyond family has become immeasurably large.

- Adolescents who appear more capable and assume an air of bravado actually feel less confident to cope with this next stage of growth.

- Adolescents who push for new freedoms cannot do so without taking new risks and creating new fears.

Because of the increasing friction and sense of distance with their son or daughter, parents do not usually welcome many of these early adolescent changes. The child who was more endearing to be around has become the adolescent who is more abrasive to live with. Thus, supporting their son or daughter as childhood ends and adolescence begins can be difficult.

The challenge of parenting an early adolescent is to do all you can to secure the young person during what is an insecure time in his or her development. By "secure" I mean that despite the young person's changes, parents act as loving, nurturing, and steadfastly committed as ever. To that end, there are some actions you can consistently take.

- Reach out and stay in positive communication with your child while adolescence is causing more tension and conflict between you.

- Be sufficiently open and supportive to allow needed experimentation and redefinition to occur within safe and respectful limits.

- Encourage the young person's friendships but insist that he or she maintain an active membership in the family.

- Provide sufficient structure and supervision to help channel new growth so that it unfolds constructively and responsibly.

- Accept that each child's adolescence will have its own unique trajectory (i.e., course of experience, speed of development, emotional intensity), so parents must work with their child and learn to play the hand they are dealt.

Hardest of all, you must let your "child" go so that he or she can begin to grow up. Your daughter can't become a young woman and remain your little girl. Your son can't become a young man and remain your little boy. In both cases, this release can be particularly agonizing for young people if childhood has been a rewarding and harmonious experience, one that they might want to protract and be reluctant to give up. For example, because they are so closely attached to parents, many only children delay beginning adolescence because the separation from childhood security is so painful to make and childhood terms feel so good the way they are. The loss for parents can be profound as well, because the onset of adolescence means you will never have your son or daughter as a little child again. The golden period in your relationship is over. It can suddenly seem as though a stranger has taken over the child you knew so well and enjoyed so much. Now you have someone very different to live with.

What you typically notice at this juncture is a *change* in your son's or daughter's energy, attitude, and behavior. Young people's energy becomes harder for them to organize: Their attitude toward life becomes more complaining; and their behavior becomes more resistant. They now become harder to happily live with, because it has become harder for them to happily live with themselves. It's an awkward time for all involved. Some of the words I hear parents use to describe the unwelcome transformation in a son or daughter this age commonly include adjectives such as *restless, irritable, inattentive, forgetful, distracted, inconsiderate, disorganized, complaining, moody, critical, irritable, argumentative, stubborn,* and *uncooperative.*

What parents are typically responding to are the three normal phases of early adolescent change that begin to now unfold: the *negative attitude, active and passive resistance,* and *early experimentation.*

Negative Attitude

First, the *negative attitude* comes to characterize the young person who has become dissatisfied and complains much of the time. These complaints often share common themes: There is nothing to do (boredom); nothing is good enough (criticism); and nothing is fair (injustice). Rejecting being defined and treated as a "child," the early adolescent develops a more negative frame of mind. Although the early adolescent knows what old definition he or she doesn't want, the young person hasn't yet figured out what new one to construct in its place. Consequently, when he or she was just a child, you (as parents) could do no wrong, but now it seems you can't do anything right. You have been knocked off the pedestal of childhood adoration and have lost approval in the adolescent's eyes. *The function of the negative attitude is to create sufficient dissatisfaction with remaining defined as a child to encourage the beginning of adolescent change.*

Active and Passive Resistance

Second, based on the grievances against parental unfairness and the desire for more self-determination, *active and passive resistance* to parental requests are now the order of the day. The young person will actively argue with anything you say, and he or she will passively delay doing whatever you want. Asking "why do I have to?" begins most arguments, and promising "I'll do it later" delays immediate compliance with most parental requests. This resistance is part of becoming more aggressive with parents to get what one wants and avoid what one doesn't want. Early adolescence is a more aggressive age, because young people must break the traditional boundaries of childhood to create more room to grow. *The function of this aggression is for adolescents to gather more power to challenge the parental authority that sets and patrols the limits of their freedom.* It is also the energy they carry into peer relationships at this age that causes them to be more combative with each other. Social cruelty is one example of this more aggressive age.

Early Experimentation

Third, because parents are often tired, busy, or insufficiently resolved, adolescent resistance succeeds in creating some freedom for *early experimentation*, testing parental and social limits to see what they can get away with. Adolescents probe the firmness of prohibitions, explore forbidden experiences, and relentlessly exploit parental inconsistency. Parental inconsistency around a rule or restraint sends a double message: "Maybe we mean it this time, or maybe we don't." The early adolescent cannot resist gambling on "maybe we don't." *The function of early experimentation is to see what rules, demands, and restraints are firm and not worth fighting, and which ones are worth challenging, because parents don't have the resolve to back them up.*

The hallmarks of early adolescence for parents are having a young person with a more negative, critical, and complaining mind-set; more active and passive aggressive energy; and more interest in testing limits for the sake of social independence. This is a more difficult son or daughter to parent than they had before.

Naturally, it is hard for parents to adjust their expectations and sensitivities to fit and support the emerging adolescent who has now become more *apathetic* ("I don't care!"), more *avoidant* ("I'll do it later!"), more *adventurous* ("I'm going to try!"), and more *argumentative* ("Why should I?"). Thus, if the onset of adolescence doesn't alienate you, it at least puts you off. This new sense of strain on your relationship contributes to the adolescent's feelings of insecurity as he or she begins the long fight to break free of your authority and finally establish true independence.

Growing up is tough, and it needs to be, because the child must toughen up to become an early adolescent who can increasingly operate on his or her social own. This includes coping with a world of peers in which there is now more back and forth, push and shove, give and take. Part of that toughening-up process begins with more conflict with parents at home and a desire to be less babied by them. Now parents become unwitting sparring partners, training the young person to manage more contested relationships with peers.

Parents as the *rule makers* find their traditional authority frequently challenged by adolescents as the *rule breakers* who are pushing for more freedom to grow. The *age of command* (when the children believed they had to do what they were told) is over, and the *age of consent* (when the adolescents realize that cooperation with a parent is up to them) has arrived. Now parents must cope with a diminished sense of influence and control. In the words of one father: "At this age, there is a lot of mouth, a lot of mess, and a lot of rolling eyes." The early adolescent questions parental decisions and criticizes their failings. No wonder parents wonder: "What has adolescence done to our child?"

The answer is *a lot*. The young person's physical and social *characteristics* have started to change. Adolescents are starting to appear and act more adult. For example, they may even ask to borrow some of your clothes that are now large enough to fit them and that they're now motivated to wear. So too, their *values* have started to change. They have developed some beliefs and priorities that run counter to yours as the parents. For example, they may now be more drawn to dark and violent entertainment that you dislike, and may also rank securing good friends above achieving good grades. Their *habits* have started to change too. They have developed patterns of conduct different from when they were children. For example, they may have become more nocturnal, inclined to stay up later at night (and become harder for you to awaken in the morning). Finally, their *wants* have started to change. The permissions they ask for are harder for parents to grant. For example, they may now want more social freedom and money to pay for it. Most parents discover that an adolescent is more expensive to financially support than a child.

Ironically, at the same time that they want *more* from their parents, they seem to want *less* to do with them. For example, the parent (often the mother) who had a very open and confiding relationship with the child now has an early adolescent who is more private and less inclined to talk with her. Or the parent (often the father) who had a very active companionship with the child now has an early adolescent who wants to do more with friends and less with him. In both cases, parents should not treat adolescent separation as a personal

repudiation, because it isn't. It is simply the adolescent rejecting childhood status and definition, and then acting out that
rejection against traditional parental treatment to make room
for more independent growth ahead. *The rejection is for personal
change and is not intended to offend or hurt the parents.*

This growing apart from parents is further complicated
by more frequent episodes of opposition. Now bravery is re-
quired on both sides, because adolescence is an act of courage.
For the young person, it is not easy to assert more individuality and independence with the most powerful people in the
world, namely the parents, insisting on his or her way when it
is often against the way of the parents or outside their understanding. This new passage for adolescents feels emotionally
costly when they have to provoke your disagreement, displea-
sure, disapproval, and even disappointment to get room to
grow. Their adolescence is not easy for parents either. You
often have to tell them what they don't want to hear as well as
make demands and set restraints they don't agree with or like.
To act responsibly, you must become unpopular with your
adolescents, taking stands for their best interests against their
urgent wants, and you will often be resented for your efforts
on their behalf. To be a good parent of an adolescent means
you cannot always act like a good friend. *The age of thankless
parenting has arrived.*

At adolescence, you have each been altered in the other's
eyes. For the parents, the child who used to be loving,

obedient, hardworking, and helpful has become the early adolescent who is often inconsiderate, resistant, unmotivated, and
moody. But ask these young people how they know that they
are now adolescents, and the evidence they will cite describes
how their parents have changed…and not for the good. You
used to be understanding, patient, trusting, and fun, and now
you are worrying, critical, questioning, and tense. So who has
changed? You both have. And because you have, the relationship between you has become harder to manage.

Although parents want their children to grow older and
become more responsible, they don't really want them to
endure the normal adolescent process that growing up requires. What they really desire is for their sons or daughters
to magically achieve independence without sacrificing any of
the old familiarity, closeness, and compliance they loved about
their childhood. Adolescence, however, requires that the young
person must contest and ultimately overthrow parental authority to claim true individuality and functional independence. To
mount such an insurrection, the young person must strain the
relationship with his or her parents. This is one reason why
early adolescence is the age of insecurity. It is the major reason why
sanctuary with peers now becomes so much more important,
peers who are all feeling more strained in their relationships
with their parents at home.

And of course, at this same time, through no choice of
their own, there is an enormous contribution made to that

insecurity by the onset of puberty, when young bodies grow out of control, with hormonal changes that signal the arrival of sexual maturity. Self-consciousness of these physical changes creates one of the most powerful vulnerabilities to social cruelty. To keep social attention off their own changes, young people attack these changes in others.

Puberty

Jesse had just about decided he was better off not speaking at all. Having his voice drop was no laughing matter, except to the other kids, that is. Now, whenever he spoke, even his friends laughed at him. And heaven forbid a teacher should call on him to answer a question in class, which his language arts teacher did almost every day to the delight of those students eager to make fun of him some more. A few of the other boys had even taken to imitating his lowered register when he was nearby. Worst of all, there was nothing he could do about this alteration. His body was in charge.

Adolescence and puberty are not the same, but they usually coincide in early adolescence. Adolescence is a ten- to twelve-year process of *social* and *psychological* growth that ends with the young person becoming responsible enough to claim *functional independence*. Puberty is a hormonally induced year-and-a-half to three-year process of *sexual* and *physical* growth that ends with the arrival of *reproductive maturity*. Like it or not, with the arrival of puberty, boys and girls change in the following ways:

- They lose their childlike bodies to sexual development.

- They undergo physical changes over which they have no control.

- They begin their respective journeys to young manhood and womanhood.

- They develop young womanly and manly ideals of appearance to identify with and strive for.

- They start sexualizing their relationship with each other in a socially awkward fashion.

Unable to govern or anticipate what is happening to their bodies, adolescents become intensely self-conscious and preoccupied by physical alterations in their appearances. Subjecting themselves to painful examination in the mirror on a daily basis to discover the latest alterations that have befallen their bodies overnight, they take a much longer time getting ready for school, where they fear public exposure of their defects may await. Now no blemish is too small for them to ignore, because they assume other people will scrutinize them as mercilessly as they do themselves. This is how puberty turns early adolescence into an age of discontent ("I hate how I look!") and susceptibility to embarrassment ("What if other people notice?"). At a time when their physical appearance becomes much more socially important, puberty makes an enormous contribution to early adolescent insecurity, because the young person feels intensely self-conscious and self-critical of the bodily changes that he or she cannot control.

To make matters worse, if maturation comes early, young people must then cope with the expectation to act the age they appear, even when they appear much older than their actual age. One eleven-year-old who looked sixteen described her insecurity: "People treat me like I'm supposed to know about and want all kinds of things I don't!" And if one is slow to mature, one can feel left behind, too. "Everybody treats me like I'm still a little kid!"

Adolescents face particular anxiety about how womanly or manly their bodies will turn out. Thus, they compare their bodies to the developing bodies of their peers, the most popular students who usually represent how everyone wants to look, and the cultural idols that model physical perfection that they can never hope to attain but feel obliged to emulate. An early adolescent boy with a sunken chest or an early adolescent girl with no discernable breasts can feel woefully deficient compared to their more "normal" friends. Most young people going through puberty are afflicted by sexual ideals that seem hopelessly out of reach; so many young women start dieting to become thin and many young men start lifting weights to put on more muscle at this age of personal discontent, both efforts testifying to the insufficiencies they feel. In the extreme, girls can start developing anorexic eating habits, and boys can start resorting to muscle building supplements. This is often when eating behaviors diverge in either of two extreme directions as growth spurts take over. One young person may decide to give up eating breakfast (often girls), and another may choose to eat all the time (often boys).

Then, of course, there is the social awkwardness of relating to the opposite sex in order to prove that the young manly or young womanly side of oneself is indeed coming out.

Becoming girl crazy or boy crazy, having a crush, and getting a "ten-minute" girlfriend or boyfriend are all less about attraction to the opposite sex than expressing social and sexual readiness to relate. Having a boyfriend or girlfriend is an important rite of passage into acting more grown-up.

And this is also the age when boys start getting interested in watching pornography and girls get interested in reading romance novels—both of which are preoccupations that distort what healthy male/female identities and relationships are really about. What these fictions portray are stereotypes: males as sexual aggressors and females as sexual attractors, arousing anxieties on both counts. (Additionally, the male-as-aggressor ideal contributes to a higher disciplinary rate for boys challenging school authority, physically acting out, and resisting schoolwork, which generally results in lower academic performance than for girls in early adolescence.) In the end, boys worry they are not aggressive enough, and girls worry they are not attractive enough.

So children this age not only feel insecure about their bodies, but they also feel insecure in comparison to same-sex peers and about not measuring up to cultural icons. Moreover, they feel uncertain about how to relate to peers across the sexual divide. As a middle school principal once flippantly described, "Boys often stay out of the bathroom for fear of being beaten up, and girls often use the bathroom when they need a good private place to cry." Boys and girls can live in the same school and manage social cruelty differently.

Sometimes, parents will get impatient with their early adolescents: "All you do is spend time looking in the mirror. All you care about is your appearance!" But parents don't understand that it is their bodies, with all their unpredictable changes, that young people have to take to school each day for all to see and some to criticize or tease. No social criticism measures up to the cruelty of self-examination and self-censure that young people subject themselves to every day.

One practical intervention that parents can make to help reduce some of puberty's upsetting effects is giving their early adolescent solid information about what puberty is, why it occurs, how it influences bodily growth, and how all young people go through it. *Parents need to normalize puberty.* Early adolescents need to know that no matter how self-conscious about becoming different they feel, none of them are experiencing anything unique. Although young people may not talk much to each other about the insecurities of the process, they are all in company with each other as they each undergo this hormonal and physical change; so you need to talk with your son or daughter about puberty, and you need to be open to answering any questions the young person may ask. If you don't feel sufficiently informed, look up *puberty* on the Internet, find a website where the information seems agreeable, sit down with your son or daughter, and then read the material together. Ignorance of puberty only adds to the insecurity of the experience; knowledge can normalize much of the process.

Sensitivity to puberty is also intensified at this age because early adolescence brings two developmental changes that significantly differentiate the young person from the child he or she was: *self-consciousness* and *social awareness*, both of which can be major contributors to social cruelty. Self-consciousness is the capacity to step back and observe oneself, critically appraise oneself, compare oneself to others, imagine how one looks in others' eyes, and become sensitive to criticism and embarrassment. Social awareness is the capacity to see other people's perspective, to see the world through their values, to become more sensitive to what it's like to be them, and to become more aware of one's impact on others. With the development of self-consciousness and social awareness, the "eyes of the world" matter as never before. *Self-consciousness makes it easier to be hurt, and social awareness makes it easier to hurt others.* It's not that children cannot be socially cruel to each other; but early adolescents are far more developmentally equipped to give and take injury with each other. A mother summed it up this way: "My child and her friends can hurt each other, but my young teenager and her friends can really treat each other mean."

There is another contribution to insecurity made by social independence, one aspect of which is feeling much more socially exposed and alone as one becomes more separated from family. If puberty only unfolded at home, that would be one thing. However, just as young people venture out into their own social world, the changes of puberty become baggage they must carry along.

Social Independence

"What's middle school like?" I asked a sixth-grade client. "Is it different from elementary school?"

He shook his head. "It's like the wild west out there," he finally said.

"Except there are still laws to follow," I argued. "The adults are still in charge." That's when he gave me that look of pity conveying how little I understood. "Tell me," I said, and he did.

"The teachers only run the classrooms. The students rule the halls."

Young people inhabit a whole new social world during their middle school years. Everyone is seeking a social place and often a group to identify with, a cohort of companions to share the growing adventures ahead. On some level, most young people seem to know that adolescence is no time to go it alone. As for the company of parents, they have become outsiders to this adolescent world—onlookers and advisors—but they are not as directly involved as they once were during the sheltered childhood years. Then their children played with each other under parental supervision, still subject to the primary influence of family values.

Come early adolescence, the rules for social interaction within this community of peers are rewritten as young people start constructing and conducting their separate social worlds. When it comes to concerns about social independence, parents tend to get preoccupied with only one half of the struggle—the young person's striving against them for more autonomy. But they do not adequately attend to the other half—how the young person is learning to treat and be treated by peers.

The middle school years are when young people feel the early impact of this new social independence most strongly, because by then virtually all of the students have entered early adolescence. What parents notice is how young people become focused on the drama of their new social world. Who is saying what about whom? Who is doing what with whom? Who is doing what to whom? Who is getting together? Who is breaking up? Who did what? Who has tried what? Who has been invited? Who has been left out? These questions attract young people's attention, curiosity, and conversation, because come social independence, the world of peers is suddenly absorbing.

In childhood, they weren't that interested in the soap opera of each other's lives, but in early adolescence, they definitely are. Even with the increasing electronic means of communication, such as computers, cell phones, and various handheld devices, it is hard to stay current with all that is happening in the social sphere. It's difficult to stay in the know. And those who don't are "out of it," at a social disadvantage, because they are not keeping up with the latest social news. For parents who wonder about their son's or daughter's interests in high social drama, social independence is the reason why, and it is from the management (or mismanagement, if you will) of social independence that mistreatment from social cruelty can arise.

Children learn the first rules for social treatment within the family under the supervision of parents. However, these adult-based rules are revised within socially independent adolescent peer groups to encourage less sensitive and considerate, more unkind and ruthless ways that often endorse acting meanly when social survival feels threatened. It is during early adolescence when young people make their declaration of independence from childhood and family. Now they want more freedom to run their social lives, and they get what they want. As a seventh grader's mom once said to me after she watched her daughter adjust from elementary school, "Middle school isn't Kansas anymore. Now these kids are socially on their own."

In these socially independent groups, there are all kinds of questions to be answered, as young people decide how to interact and *learn* how to treat each other. For example, adolescents will ask themselves how they should treat the following peers and various groups:

- Who they like

- Who are like them

- Who they want to be like

- Who they want to like them

- Who they simply don't like

- Whose treatment they don't like

- Who are disliked by people they like

- Who they don't want to be like

- Who they know don't like them

If parents and teachers leave young people alone to figure out the rules of social conduct at this sensitive and impressionable time, they allow social cruelty to reign free. Respecting the early adolescent need for social independence can be good for parents, too; however, abandoning young people to define and manage how they should treat each other with their newfound social independence is not. As adolescents jockey for social position and ascendancy, good kids are in danger of treating each other badly to feel better or keep from getting hurt. Unchecked, even good children can start believing that this mistreatment is okay. Hence, when a son comes home and tells his parent what he thinks is a proud story about how he and his buddies were able to gang up on a student they didn't like and keep him from joining their group, the parent has to say, "How you manage your world of friends is up to you, but just so you know, I disagree with what you did. Boasting about outnumbering, excluding, and hurting somebody seems like a sad way to feel good. Surely, if you don't want someone to join your group, there is a kinder way to let that be known."

When personal worth, desire for belonging, feelings of competence, social identity, and sense of purpose all depend on a group or gang of friends, then the adolescent has become a captive of his or her independent company of peers. This is why parents need to listen when their son or daughter says, "My friends are all that matter to me. They are everything!" That's the time to get their early adolescent more involved in family, more connected to other salient adults, and enrolled in outside activities.

Early adolescents definitely need the companionship of peers, but at the same time, they must remain rooted in their family in ways that nourish their sense of worth, belonging, competence, and purpose. This is why the attachment and connection to parents is so important and why abandonment by parents can be so devastating. *Being detached and disconnected from parents at this juncture unduly increases reliance on a "family" of peers, often to a socially cruel effect.*

So what can parents do to help their sons or daughters at such a tumultuous time in their lives? The answer is *a lot.*

Consider how you can moderate the insecurities of autonomy, puberty, and social independence that have been discussed so far in the book.

What Parents Can Do

The first task for parents when early adolescence begins is to *accept* the child's separation from childhood and the changes that come with it. The second task for parents is to be *sensitive* to the insecurity that develops as childhood is let go and lost, as relations to parents become more strained, and as the challenge of peer belonging becomes more daunting. The third task for parents is to stay actively *connected* with the child while the child is distancing him or herself, because that family connection is the greatest antidote to insecurity.

Separation does not have to result in disconnection from parents, but requires that they keep reaching out. *It has been my experience that young people who feel accepted by parents and feel actively connected to them as early adolescence separation unfolds are less likely to engage in social cruelty for survival and are less severely impacted when this mistreatment comes their way.*

Though parents and children may feel compatible, much of that sense of easy fit is lost come adolescence. Now, the adolescent feels he or she has less in common with family and more in common with peers. As a result, what to do with parents and what to say to them may feel more awkward than before. Thus, companionship and communication become more of a challenge. When the adolescent starts growing up and moving away from childhood, he or she starts growing away from parents and family, too.

When the young person's increasing autonomy leads to more isolation in the family, it can encourage the adolescent to compensate for this loss of parental and family connection by placing undue social importance on relationships with peers. Those parents who take offense at normal early adolescent separation and treat it as a rejection by rejecting back will foster more insecurity. Instead, the parents' job is to do what they can to stay connected to the young person while adolescence runs its course. To accomplish these tasks, four attitude adjustments can ease a parent's way:

- *Don't take your child's adolescence personally.* Your son or daughter is not "doing this" to get back at you or get you upset. Adolescents do it *for* themselves, for personal growth, unmindful of their parents. They are too self-centered to think about the effects of their development on the rest of the family. Put other adults in your place, and your son or daughter would still be going through the same changes.

- *Don't treat adolescence as a punishable offense.* It is a process of growth. Accept the process, but hold the young person responsible for the choices he or she makes as the process unfolds. Accept that the adolescent will become more argumentative, but still hold him or her accountable for *how* he or she chooses to manage this disputive communication.

- *Understand that adolescence wears the magic out of parenting.* Once entranced by the one-year-old who was so entranced with them, ten years later, parents are offended by the eleven-year-old who is now more offended by them. The function of this mutual disenchantment is to wear down the dependence adolescents have on their parents, allowing more independence to grow as a result.

- *Accept that teenagers are naturally offensive.* Healthy adolescents push for all the freedom they can get as soon as they can get it; and healthy parents restrain that push in the interest of safety and responsibility. This is the conflict of interests that unfolds over the course of adolescence, only ending when the young people assume full authority and responsibility for directing their lives.

When parents can adopt attitudes like these, it enables them to act more rational and accepting, as well as less emotional and critical. Remember how the early adolescent is thrown into a world of experience with peers where social upheaval and peer rejection are a daily possibility, where, for example, your daughter's best friend yesterday may not speak to her today or may even side against her. This uncertainty makes it imperative for parents to keep in mind that just because their child is separating from them does *not* mean that he or she no longer needs to be connected to them. On the contrary, adolescents need a strong connection with parents more than ever during this socially insecure and lonely time in order to steady themselves. As friendships become more unstable and fickle, parents and family need to provide the constancy of acceptance and belonging on which the young person can securely depend.

Simply because the adolescent has become more distant is no reason for parents to become distant in return—no more than the adolescent becoming more critical is an excuse for parents to become more critical, too. Independence from parents must not mean isolation from parents. Their task is to do all they can to keep the relationship with their son or daughter strong while adolescence is now causing them to start growing apart. To this end, they must keep up *constant contact and communication*. They have to counter the normal increased adolescent separation and involvement with peers by maintaining the *three initiatives for family involvement* at home:

- Invitation

- Inclusion

- Insistence

Invitation means that parents must continually invite the young person to do activities with them and to talk with them. Every time they make such an initiative, parents create a choice point for the adolescent to accept, reject, or put on hold for later use. In situations in which the child didn't need many invitations to get involved with parents, and even initiated many invitations of his or her own, the adolescent is placed in an uncomfortable position, feeling unable to give as many invitations to and accept as many invitations from parents. However, this does not mean that the adolescent isn't as much in need of connecting with parents, only that now he or she finds it more difficult to do so. Parents just need to reach out more often, avoid feeling rejected when rebuffed, and resolve themselves to maintain that initiative through thick and thin, good times and bad. A mother who had a confiding child may have a more private adolescent. A father who had an eager companion for a child may have an adolescent more interested in spending time with friends. Does this mean that parents should neglect the time to talk and do things with their children? No! But it does mean that these times may be harder to find, so parents have to keep trying, not get discouraged, and catch the young person when, for whatever reason, he or she is momentarily available for communication and companionship.

Inclusion means that the adolescent is expected to participate in any significant family routines, gatherings, special events, celebrations, and traditions. These specific experiences have symbolic value because joining in these observances represents the young person's active membership in his or her primary social group. This participation is not an invitation to accept or decline; it is an expectation to be met. Inclusion affirms a base of social belonging that existed before an adolescent peer group came into being, one that will continue long after that peer group has served its passing purpose and disappeared.

Insistence means that the adolescent is supposed to contribute unpaid chores to help support family functioning. This participation is not an invitation or an expectation; it is a requirement. It too has symbolic value, because such contributions demonstrate commitment to the family. Chores are some of the dues of family membership that everyone, even adolescents, must pay. By supporting the family, the young person feels connected to the family, even though he or she may complain about chores that can often get in the way of fun. "Why should I do work for the family?" she may ask, to which parents need to reply, "Because families take a lot of work and everyone must share the load."

A corollary to this insistence on housework is the importance of insisting on the accomplishment of schoolwork. At this age, the early adolescent's apathy (loss of traditional caring) that enabled the separation from childhood can discount the old importance of faithfully completing his or her studies and doing well in school on the grounds that he or she is no longer a child. But school performance is connected to self-worth, because doing well can influence one's self-esteem. So parents understand this motivational dip. They can understand how the child cared about doing well in school, how the early adolescent often cares less about doing well in school, and how the late adolescent will care about doing well in school once again. Thus, parents can say something like this should their early adolescent's achievement drop: "We know you used to care about achieving in school, and right now, it feels like it matters less. We also know that in a few years it will matter to you more. While you are going through a time when you care less about your studies, we will care enough to supervise you more to help maintain adequate performance. This way, when you are older and the benefits of achieving well matter again, you will be able to do as well as you want."

Not only do parents need to keep early adolescents tied to the family while they separate from their childhoods, parents also need to stay connected as their children differentiate how they were as children from how their parents have traditionally known them. Now parents can find it difficult to accept and understand the new forces that are shaping their children's changing interests, associations, and identity. These differences can seem so unfamiliar and unappealing—the harsh music that now blasts from their rooms, for example—that they can start feeling estranged from the son or daughter who used to feel more compatible and comfortable to be around. Consider the world of differences between the innocent videos and computer games that entertained children and the hard-edged, violent games that adolescents now find so absorbing. In response, parents may either insist that the young person return to old enjoyments that they once shared together or they may criticize what captures their son's or daughter's interest and attention now. Either response can be alienating at a time when the adolescent is already pulling away, serving only to increase his or her belief that friends can understand how he or she has changed.

In this independent world, not only peers but also popular media play an influential role in shaping the young person's growth by providing new images, expressions, icons, values, and activities with which to experiment and identify. What's exciting? What's new? What's cool? What's in? What's latest? What's manly? What's womanly? The marketplace, fashion, and the media decide. And since parents can't keep all these influences out, they must keep up with those that come in to stay current with their adolescent.

It is *not* the adolescent's job to maintain commonality with parents as he or she grows. Young people's job is to differentiate themselves from the child they were as they search for their new, more grown-up identity. It is the parents' job to keep reaching out to establish commonality with the adolescent as he or she changes so they can stay connected. *Bridging differences with interest* is how this is done, so rather than act offended by the latest fad that has caught their adolescent's attention, parents can try the following acts to connect with their son or daughter:

- Express curiosity

- Show a desire to be taught

- Make an effort to understand

- See if there are ways to become involved

Parents may also try asking bridge-building questions, such as:

- "Can you help me understand?"

- "Will you show me how it is done?"

- "Would you tell me more about it?

- "Could I come along, stay out of the way, and watch?"

Asking your child to explain something to you creates a very powerful reversal. The young person is placed in a superior position of authority that allows him or her to teach parents about his or her world of experience, and the parents are in the subordinate position of students wanting to be enlightened. In this position, adolescents feel treated with respect, not as an opponent but as a valued informant. Teaching one's parents translates respect from them into esteem for oneself; the adolescent has something the parents consider *worth* learning. This is truly a win-win arrangement. By bridging adolescent differences with their interest, parents remain connected with their growing son or daughter.

At this age, the social influence of peers now competes with the family influence of the parents, against whom most early adolescent separation is acted out. The outcome of this rivalry is often complicated: When the two sources of influence conflict, young people may act according to what their friends dictate rather than what parents have taught. Thus, as peer influence rises, parental influence falls. In the extreme cases, early adolescents can encourage a troublemaking ethic in each other, one with an emphasis on rejection (of childhood), rebellion (against authority), and rule breaking (to see what they can get away with). If peers are the only influence that matter, then peers matter way too much, and the role of parents and other adults to encourage more maturity and responsibility has been lost.

However, parents can shift the odds in the favor of mature guidance by enrolling other salient adults into the young person's life. (By "salient," I mean other adults who matter to the young person and whom the young person values and respects.) Their child's early adolescence is no time for parents to socially abandon a more distant, disaffected, and resistant young person to the culture and company of peers. Separation from parents is natural, but age segregation among peers is not. In fact, this is a time for parents to increase their own and other adults' involvement in the early adolescent's life to compensate for the shortsighted influence of peers.

By enlisting other adults whom the young person looks up to and identifies with, parents can—through these surrogates—encourage the young person's positive growth of responsibility, desire for competence, willingness to confide, and ability to develop constructive interests. Just because an early adolescent is having a hard time connecting with parents, this does not mean that he or she cannot connect with these other adults. And just because the young person is usually more positive to them than to his or her parents is no reason for parents to feel devalued, threatened, resentful, or jealous. In fact, parents should be grateful their young teenagers are open to guidance from other salient adults that they cannot accept from their parents at the moment.

Salient adults may be found among older siblings, members of the extended family, long-standing friends of the family, special activity instructors and coaches, youth leaders and mentors, as well as significant teachers at school. At this age, young people can often attach to the mother or father of a close friend, treating this adult as a second parent, the home as a place for second family. A parent's job at this juncture is to expand the field of salient adult associations so that these older connections can nourish and direct the young person's growth in ways that can counterbalance and complement the influence of peers.

As early adolescents claim a stronger affiliation with peers in search of more social independence and cultural kinship, parents who once felt so primary in their children's lives can start to feel peripheral, pushed to the outside. These young people would rather spend more time with friends than parents and family. Now, adolescents have become less confiding with their parents and more preoccupied with being in constant communication with peers. In consequence, parents can feel like they are losing a social competition. Even worse, they can fear that the influence of these peer associations is leading their son or daughter astray from family values, especially as peer pressure grows and parental influence seems to wane. If parents have little to no contact with these friends, they can also start to fear for the worst and see these new friends as the enemy of the child they love.

What to do? The answer is simple: Do *not* turn your child's friends into your enemies. You will frighten yourselves by imagining fearful possibilities from the association. You will reduce your influence by acting hostile toward the friends. You will increase your adolescent's attachment to his or her friends in their defense. And you will alienate both your child and his or her friends by your suspicion and opposition. By your rejecting their friends, adolescents will feel that you are rejecting them as well. Like this young person who exploded at her parents said, "If you don't like my friends, then you don't like me! I am my friends!" So the answer is simple: Get to know your adolescent's friends. Welcome them into your family. Become an adult friend to your son's or daughter's friends.

The more your son's or daughter's friends feel at home in your home, comfortable, and close with you, the more connected your adolescent will feel with you. Their friendliness toward you will accredit you in the eyes of your adolescent. In addition, as they become more known, they will become less frightening to you. As you find ways to enjoy them, they will enjoy you, and that will give you an influential connection with them, because they will factor their relationship with you into their relationship with your adolescent. Many adolescents at this age are open to surrogate parents. They may value interest and caring from you that is hard to accept from their own parents at the moment, much in the same way your child may be attaching to some of their parents.

■ ■ ■

In summary, early adolescence (around ages nine to thirteen) begins the separation from childhood that creates the *developmental insecurity*, sense of *personal vulnerability*, and challenge of more *social independence* with which young people must now contend. At this phase, there is a heightened need for attachment and acceptance in a more independent and unstable society of peers who are feeling insecure and vulnerable, too. It is this potent mix of insecurity, vulnerability, and need for social belonging in a more independent world of peers that I believe is the cradle for social cruelty.

When adolescents reach this age, parents must do everything they can to keep themselves and the young person well connected, because the strength of that connection is the best bulwark against giving or taking pain as a result of social cruelty that I have seen. The best prevention is parental connection. When parents and young people remain well attached and in good communication during the transition into early adolescence, the primary causes of social cruelty—insecurity, vulnerability, and the compensatory need for peer belonging—have limited effect.

Frequently, the first evidence that children have entered the age of social cruelty is when they start treating people at home with meanness, such as calling younger siblings by degrading names or making fun of other family members. What parents observe and report is something like the following: "He has started treating the younger kids so meanly...and sometimes us." This is a fairly reliable sign that relationships at school have now turned socially cruel. Feeling bad about him or herself, an early adolescent starts acting like it's okay to treat other people badly too, especially as it is increasingly happening among his or her peers. In response, parents need to confront and correct the new behavior. "This may be how you and your friends treat each other at school now; but I want you to know I don't agree with this conduct, and I will not allow you to act this way at home." At home, the rules for respectful communication and considerate conduct must apply.

As parents, your final job is to address the symptoms of social cruelty and the actual tactics used. You must help your early adolescent refrain from engaging in these behaviors and learn how to cope when becoming a target of such mistreatment. Parents who show that they know about the hard side of social life can encourage a young person to become more open to the idea of confiding his or her experiences and perhaps even become more willing to seek parental advice and support should the need arise.

Each of the following five chapters describes a major tactic of social cruelty. Each operationally defines what that tactic is, explains some of the psychology that makes it work and hurt, and then presents some suggestions about what parents can do to help their child deal with this behavior. The next chapter begins this examination by discussing teasing.

CHAPTER THREE

TEASING

S he didn't make it; she was born with it—her nose. And in elementary school that was okay. How she was treated was based on how she acted, not how she looked. But now in seventh grade, when appearance counted for so much, sometimes other girls would tease, "What's the matter, Blaise? You having a bad nose day?" Looking in the mirror before school, she could always see what they were making fun of. Her nose looked big for her face. One day, a girl who she had beaten out for a starting spot on the basketball team threw the nickname "Snout" at her. Some of the girl's friends picked it up, and the name stuck. Blaise acted like she didn't care, but as she started to hate her nose, she started to hate herself.

The first major tactic of social cruelty to discuss is teasing. *Teasing* is the use of words to pick on or ridicule some aspect of another person about which he or she feels self-conscious, vulnerable, or insecure. The purpose is to put the person down in the teaser's eyes, the eyes of witnesses, and often in his or her own. Teasing is insulting with intent to hurt. It targets the insecurities of the person by the following methods:

- By picking on *relationship,* the teaser succeeds in making the other person feel socially embarrassed. "Who's your dorky friend?"

- By picking on *performance,* the teaser succeeds in making the other person feel defensive. "You're really good at giving wrong answers!"

- By picking on *appearance,* the teaser succeeds in making the other person feel worthless. "If I was as fat as you, I'd dress in a blanket!"

In these cases, the teaser seeks to contrast him or herself to something inferior or unattractive about the person teased. The payoff for the teaser is a feeling of superiority based on the comparison made. A middle school student put it perfectly: "If I can look down on someone that puts me above them and makes me better."

The Psychology of Teasing

A major vulnerability to cruelty in early adolescence is the insecurity that growing out of childhood creates.

What might one be insecure about? The answer is all aspects of becoming *different* that can now be painfully apparent in a world of peers who are also feeling insecure about their development. At this age, young people fear public attention to the slightest awkwardness, ignorance, blemish, inadequacy, frailty, mistake, or shortcoming. From a lingering aspect of childhood (still enjoying TV kid shows) to an unsuccessful effort at mastery (getting a classroom answer wrong) to an unwelcome sign of puberty (one's voice dropping), adolescents feel in constant danger of having some awkwardness or ineptitude about them publicly exposed.

The appearance of being "different" from peers can be a lightning rod for teasing, and most young people know how the connection works. Being different equals standing out, which equals not fitting in, which in turn equals becoming an easy target for the kind of verbal attack that teasing does. Teasing inflicts the most damage when the victim believes that the degrading statement is true and thus feels justly accused. The young person may think:

- *They're right! I will always be fat!*

- *They're right! I'm nothing but clumsy!*

- *They're right! I'm so different I'm weird!*

- *They're right! I'll never be pretty!*

- *They're right! I'll never talk right!*

When teasing is taken as truth, esteem plummets and loathing of self and anger at others can begin to build. For example, the sixth-grade boy who despairs about his diminutive size because the larger boys have taken to calling him "shortstop" may start taking his anger out on younger siblings in the family.

Teasing makes it painful to be different from one's peers, and it catches the early adolescent in a quandary. At home, young people want to differentiate themselves from how they were as children. Thus, they can even be glad when a parent notices parts of their transformation with disapproval. For example, parental impatience with how much time a female adolescent now spends grooming her appearance demonstrates how much she has changed. She spends much longer getting ready to go out because she is no longer just a child. She wants to look older to be like her friends. She wants to be "different" the same way they are. So it's okay to be different and offend your parents, but it is not okay to be different and invite teasing from friends. *She wants to resemble her peers in order to be liked by them.* For this reason, appearing different and standing out from the group norm carries the risk of not fitting in. This is why an attractive physical appearance, approved social image, and fashionable dress are so important, not to mention having the latest rage, excelling in what others do well, and being in the know about what's current. These signify that the young person is keeping up with what is "in" and "cool" and "now." They affect social membership. Apparent diversity from others can feel isolating. In the words of a seventh-grade book-lover who goes to a school where sports are all important, "People make fun of me because I'm not a jock. Not even close!"

Early adolescence is the age of intolerance. It's the fear of being different that causes early adolescents to be so critical of traits in themselves and in others who are considered socially undesirable in the culture of their peers. *Teasing ridicules a detrimental difference in a person, singling him or her out and setting him or her apart.* Teasing makes fun of something about someone that is supposedly excessive ("You're too scared! You're too slow!") or deficient ("You don't know that? You can't do that?") but unacceptable in any case. For the girl who is teased for being physically mature or the boy who is teased for being physically immature, having to suit up for physical education or extracurricular sports can be a nightmare. It feels like putting one's physical vulnerability on public display and inviting ridicule that one wishes to escape.

Simply put, at an age when part of the developmental task for adolescents is differentiating themselves from their childhood identities and consequently fitting in less with family, there is a social horror of being too different from peers.

The Power of Teasing

Teasing is always comparative and critical. It compares the person teased to the teaser who has criticized the difference.

("You don't know anything!") Teasing also is an act of social dominance, a way to literally "put someone down" to a level of social standing lower than oneself. ("Is that the best you can do?")

Teasing is more freely given to those outside one's group than inside, because within one's clique, there are rules that govern teasing. In every close-knit group, there is a social pecking order that teasing helps preserve. Therefore, adolescents tease those below to keep them in their place, but they don't tease those above and gamble with their social standing by offending highers-up. In a clique, teasing from above is often taken without complaint or teasing back. In this way, it helps define the social order. At its most offensive and provocative is the teasing that is intended and taken as personally dishonoring.

Boys will talk "smack" to each other to show how tough they are, trading insults, boasts, and threats. Girls will "flame" each other with accusations, slurs, and rumors. In either case, however, teasing may bring about violence when someone feels intolerably maligned. A major source of fights at this age is being "dissed" (i.e., being treated with deliberate *disrespect*). Insulting teasing is how this is done—attacking other people with insults about themselves, their boyfriends, their girlfriends, or their family. Let someone disrespect an adolescent, and he or she will feel dishonored at an age when personal honor may be the most reliable support for the young person's fragile self-esteem. Consequently, honor can be an issue well worth fighting for. During early adolescence, young people will fight to defend their good name when it has been disrespected. "You take that back!" demanded an eighth grader whose mother another boy had just called a "whore." When teasing takes the form of such a verbal attack, physical hostilities can break out. A veteran assistant principal who had refereed the aftermath of many of these fights once explained to me, "For a lot of these kids, acting proud is all they have to hold themselves together, to feel okay. That's why a serious insult is met with force. It's like a slap in the face. You just don't take it."

Other common expressions of disrespect include the following:

- When people act superior to someone (snobbery)

- When people talk behind someone's back (backstabbing)

- When people are dishonest to someone or about someone (lying)

- When people put someone down (ridicule)

- When people turn against someone (betrayal)

Parents don't tend to associate a sense of honor with early adolescence, but when all other avenues of affirmation and sense of worth have momentarily fallen away, honor may be the only source of pride that remains. Short of such serious insult, just being teased for being different can cause significant injury, too.

The Threat of Being "Different"

The threat of being teased for being "different" can have extensive effects. Years ago, I was in a middle school where approximately five popular and dominant seventh graders were all borderline passing students, committed to getting by with minimal effort, perhaps to show how teachers (and presumably parents) lacked the authority to make them work any harder and do any better. In response, many students who otherwise would have achieved higher grades suppressed their performance to avoid incurring the disapproval of this powerful clique by violating its performance norm. Other students didn't want to get teased and singled out for acting "too smart" and maybe suffer further consequences to their own social good. As one young man said, "If I did better, they'd get on me for trying to act better than them. They'd call me a 'school boy.'"

Two liberating questions that teachers began to ask students who were following along and suppressing potential achievement in order to avoid being teased were these:

- "How would you perform differently if you were not afraid of being teased?"

- "How do you end up feeling after underperforming out of fear?"

Teachers reported that the results for those students who were able to honestly answer these questions were that they would rather fulfill themselves than give in to the social disapproval of the "big five's" extortionate power. In the words of one teacher, "For some of these kids this was a good a lesson. 'Don't let other people set limits on what you want to achieve just because it's better than what they can or want to do.'"

In both cases, these questions helped students assess how much freedom of affirmative choice they were sacrificing to fear and how diminishing it felt to make that sacrifice. For the concerned adults, parents, and teachers, the situation was a powerful illustration of the social damage teasing can cause—and that damage can be done verbally or nonverbally.

Most teasing is verbal through the use of words intended to make fun of someone. "Sticks and stones will break my bones, but words can never hurt me" is one of those adages that sounds right but is actually wrong. In fact, words do most of the damage in all five kinds of social cruelty. Like other animals, human beings do most of their fighting with their mouths, although instead of using teeth to wound, they use words to bite. Young people who are fast on the verbal draw and accurate with the verbal shot tend to easily intimidate others, and they are usually effective at parrying any teasing that comes their way. For a physically small boy, having an arsenal of clever verbal responses can be a great equalizer. Other people are reluctant to tease a peer who has the power of cutting words, because they don't want to be teased and humiliated in return. A fast mouth—verbal quickness, cleverness, and fluency—is respected. As one young man said: "I'm quick with a comeback, so not many people try to cut me down." Unhappily, young people who are not verbally adept, who are socially shy, who think deliberately or slowly, who have a speech impediment, or who are learning English as a second language can become easy targets, because they are unlikely to tease back. They are verbally undefended.

Additionally, paying close attention to what is said becomes extremely important in middle school as young people practice more grown-up language skills. Partly from watching put-down humor in adult comedy shows and cartoons on television, they learn to use these tactics with each other. Among students, language use becomes infinitely more subtle and complex in their interactions than it was in elementary school. Now, it is full of double messages, hidden meanings, insulting compliments, and popular references that you could be ridiculed for missing, because you "just don't get it." To be put down in front of others and not know it (or not know how to respond) can be the ultimate put-down. Victims don't know what exactly the other students are laughing about, only that they're laughing at them. They may be told that they dress just like some celebrity they've barely heard of, which they may take as a compliment—that is until all the other girls laugh, because it turns out she's famous for her bad taste in clothes. So victims feel clueless about what just came down.

As for nonverbal teasing, that is done through mimicry, imitating how the victim acts in exaggerated terms, such as physical gestures, facial expressions, vocal accents, or manners of speech. Students who are often cut down because they lack quick comebacks take satisfaction in teasing another student by mimicking his or her halting speech. They may be expressively slow, but at least they're not that slow! How cruel is that?

■ ■ ■

The biggest problem with teasing, though, is that unlike the other four common social cruelty tactics (bullying, rumoring, excluding, and ganging up), which are all clearly mean in their intent, the motivation of teasing can sometimes be hard to determine. For example, after a mocking remark, the teaser says to the person teased, who has taken offense, "You don't have to act so upset. I was just kidding about how much you eat. Can't you take a joke?" How is the person being teased to know if the hurt received was accidentally inflicted or subversively intended? How is the victim to know if he or she is really being oversensitive? Now the victim feels doubly teased for not only taking the insult seriously, but for overreacting and lacking a sufficient sense of humor. A euphemism for teasing is "making fun" of somebody by making painful insults sound funny. Humor is often used to mask the hurt intended by making it entertaining to say. To the adolescents teased, if they can't laugh along with the insult then that just shows something additionally wrong with them. They have no sense of fun or humor. They are oversensitive. They are too serious. Now one can be teased for not being able to take the teasing.

The distinction for young people to make is between *friendly teasing* that is meant to express liking and be taken as fun, good-natured, and playful, and *mean teasing* that is given and taken as hostile, mean-spirited, and hurtful, intended to inflict injury. It is mean teasing that becomes a vehicle for social cruelty. Even with friendly teasing, however, young people need to be careful, lest they go too far and hurt someone they care about. The best rule for keeping teasing friendly is this: *If it is not fun for the person being teased, then it's not funny and should be stopped.* So the reply to the mocking friend should be as follows: "Well, what you said in fun at lunch about my eating hurt my feelings, so please don't say that again."

More than the other forms of social cruelty, mean teasing encourages response in kind. It tends to teach others how to mean tease back as a result. For example, among a competitive group of male peers, it is easy for teasing to become excessive. It is common for early adolescent boys, in the course of jockeying for position, to get into a *play of put-downs* that can be hard to stop once it has begun. Then, the verbal push and shove of friendly competition goes too far, and cutting words start doing hurt. However, acting tough feels more important than admitting injury, so everyone retaliates instead of backing off as an escalating game of one-upmanship begins: "Can you give it? Can you take it? Can you give it back?" What started out as funny quickly becomes less fun when hanging out together turns into a time when, as one young man put it: "We all watch out." And when ridicule and insults lead to physical encounters, it is a sign that friends have let teasing go too far. For example, a group of good male friends who hung out together often found themselves getting more and more physical with each other as aggressive words led to more "push and shove" than any of them wanted, but none felt they could afford to stop. In this case, one of them complained to the school counselor about the escalation in the course of discussing something else. Then the counselor was able to convene with the whole group and help them re-norm how they were treating each other by "cooling the taunts and insults" and getting back to keeping their friendship "fun."

Mean teasing is not meant to convey affection, amuse the person teased, help someone lighten up, laugh at him or herself, or stop taking him or herself too seriously. Mean teasing is an act of social cruelty that can serve a variety of malicious purposes:

- To set the person teased apart
- To ridicule and laugh at someone
- To criticize and put someone down
- To contrast the teaser and the teased
- To wound someone with mean words

- To label someone with a painful name

- To create a victim who gets most of the teasing

- To influence someone to act like or go along with the teaser

- To provoke a response with an insult to get someone's attention

- To verbally dominate someone to claim or defend social position

- To feel better by causing the person teased to feel worse

Teasing is a weapon that serves many social purposes, and although, like other kinds of social cruelty, teasing is an aggressive act, it is often more defensive than it seems.

■ ■ ■

Young people often tease first to prevent being teased. The teasers want to "get" others before others get them. Teasing this way is *preemptive*. It can also be *protective* when the teasers attack insecurities that they fear being teased about themselves.

Teasing someone about being a "sissy" or "wimp" among boys this age is a prime example of putting an "unmanly" label on another person that the teaser fears others will place on him, especially at an age when his sense of masculinity is extremely fragile. Comparable for a girl, she may be teased about failing to fit the young, womanly ideal of being thin enough. Now she may get teased for being heavy by other girls who themselves are afraid of appearing "fat." Teasing dehumanizes the person teased when it reduces the social worth of an individual to one negative trait. This can lead to reductionist thinking in the people teased, who allow the negative term to totally define themselves in their own minds. This is why parents have to watch for "nothing but" statements by their early adolescent. "I am nothing but a loser!" (after failing to get selected). "I am nothing but a slob!" (after being jostled at lunch and carrying a clothing stain for the rest of the school day). In each case, some teasing exploited the unhappy event. Parents need to weigh in on this reductionist thinking and tell their adolescent, "Everyone is larger than any single trait or part of their experience. An aspect of appearance or an unhappy event does not define a person. Treat yourself as if it does, and you will make yourself miserable. What happens in the moment or in response to part of you, even though you were teased about it, doesn't have to last forever. To keep the hurt of being teased from lasting, you must learn to let the teasing go."

Teasing can isolate by reducing social association. Others can easily fear being teased and isolated for hanging around or befriending the "sissy" boy or "gross" girl. At school, a young person may even elect to avoid socializing with a good friend who is the butt of constant teasing, only honoring their friendship outside of school, beyond the social scrutiny of the teasers.

Make a list of all these traits that young people tease each other about, and what you will have is a portrait of early adolescent insecurity in all its painful detail:

- Appearance

- Dress

- Degree of physical maturity and immaturity

- Departure from the dominant feminine or masculine ideal

- Possessions

- Performance

- Lack of knowledge and experience

- Family

- Heritage or culture

Cruel teasing can hurt in two serious ways: It can embarrass with humiliation, and it can isolate with shame. What most teasers do not fully understand is the depth of hostility—even enmity—that they can arouse in the victim of relentless teasing. They are surprised when someone who has quietly "taken it" without speaking up, objecting, or fighting back suddenly lashes out in vengeful violence. Relentless teasing can result in deep resentment. However, the more common damage from extreme teasing is interpersonal reservation, (i.e., the victim resorting to personal concealment and social distancing for self-protection). Now distrust and guardedness may interfere with the development of close and intimate relationships later in life. This is how painful teasing can be formative. Naturally, the victim takes protective measures to avoid being similarly hurt in the future. And teasing can be most damaging when it takes the form of *name calling*.

Name Calling

Consider the following derogatory names: *zits, hots, sleaze, skank, wimp, wuss, four-eyes, brace-face, nasty, flabs, goofus, lamebrain, weirdo, wacko, blimpy, oddball, loser, brainless,* and last but not least, *slob*.

Nicknaming is powerful because it makes insults stick. The trait that is attacked becomes a label that is attached, a term by which one is addressed and socially known.

"How do I lose my nickname?" a new girl wanted to know, feeling helpless about getting rid of the sexual nickname "easy" and the undeserved reputation that went with it. "At the very least," I suggested, "don't answer to it when someone is trying to get your attention. Wait until they use your given name. And if those you value as true friends ever slip into using your painful nickname, ask them not to do so, because it hurts and because you have a perfectly good name they can use." So the young woman spoke to her four good friends individually, and two things happened. First, they stopped using the name, and second, they confronted the other people using the name and told them to stop. Friendship was affirmed, and name calling was diminished.

The most destructive teasing uses *hate names* in the form of prejudicial terms meant to demean and dehumanize someone based on membership in some identifiable group. This kind of name calling can take the form of sexual, cultural, economic, racial, ethnic, or religious slurs—the most potentially destructive teasing of all. The problem of calling someone by a hate name is that it loads the teasing up with stereotypes that negatively define the person teased. "She's dumb like the rest!" "He's lazy like them all!" "You can't trust their kind!" "They're nothing but trash!" Because the hate names used in teasing are emotionally loaded terms, they can fuel other forms of social cruelty, such as rumoring, exclusion, bullying, and ganging up. For example, the immigrant students who may have spoken English with difficulty and with an accent were stigmatized by resident students as being stupid, inferior, and undeserving. Residents came up with a derisive name that derogated the new students' outsider statuses, their different ways, and their illiteracy with the dominant language. They started calling these immigrant students "lingos" for the strange language the residents thought they spoke. Then they blamed the lingos for "bringing the school down." Calling someone by a hate name immediately creates an us-them distinction between the supposedly superior name callers and the supposedly inferior nature of the person named. Because they are prejudicial, hate names are often used to justify mistreatment and discrimination against a person.

At worst, hate names are what I think of as "trigger terms," because they are loaded with so much animosity that the hateful names can motivate hateful actions. The inflammatory label can spark violent treatment.

At middle school, if hateful beliefs and hate naming are not addressed by resident adults and are allowed to become a normal part of the early adolescent's social world, come high school this permission may enable the development of hate-based groups. These social groups are partly organized in opposition to those individuals considered inferior, undeserving, subversive, immoral, dangerous, or impure. Members could commit hate crimes to affirm identity, claim solidarity, act out beliefs, and fulfill a sense of social purpose and superiority. For example, when gay baiting is allowed in middle school, as insecure boys tease other boys about appearing insufficiently "manly" by calling them "homo," "fag," or "queer," this can lead to the gay bashing present in some high schools. In order to define and defend their masculinity, older teenagers may beat up someone who has been labeled with a gay hate name, because he exemplifies the unmanliness they fear. To help forestall the possibility of this or any other kind of later hate attack, adults in middle school must help young people create social systems that are accepting and even welcoming of significant human differences—be they sexual, racial, functional, cultural, ethnic, economic, or religious.

This instructional initiative is vital to implement during middle school when young people are growing through an age of insecurity and vulnerability, and tend to be particularly threatened by (and intolerant of) diversity in themselves and others. Part of their new social independence as early adolescents is redefining their code for treating each other. Unless adults weigh in with ethical guidance, the cruel rules of social survival will prevail.

Puberty and Teasing

It's hard for adolescents to feel confident and normal when their bodies are transforming and going through changes they did not anticipate and cannot control. These changes include more emotional sensitivity and times of intensity, which can peak unexpectedly in ways parents do not always appreciate. "Give your hormones a break," says one dad. "Take it easy and calm down," says a mom. They don't know, or at least remember, what going through puberty is like.

For most young people, puberty (the process one's body undergoes to become sexually mature) brings many unanticipated physical changes that feel unwelcome, awkward, and potentially embarrassing. It's frightening to feel out of control of one's body, and the social consequences can be profound. Through no decisions of their own, young people are becoming physically different during an age of intolerance when everyone is extremely self-conscious and afraid of standing out by not fitting in, vulnerable to all manner of social torment on this account.

Puberty signifies that the journey to young manhood or young womanhood has begun. Now expected to develop a culturally idealized physical appearance and gender role, young people face a huge new challenge of self and social redefinition. Changes from sexual maturation (as well as the lack of those changes) can devastatingly increase exposure to teasing.

Girls can be teased for not appearing womanly enough— too undeveloped or too fat. Boys can be teased for not acting manly enough—too small or too uncoordinated. At this time, girls have enormous *appearance anxiety*, and boys have enormous *performance anxiety*. Both sexes suffer from sexual stereotypes applied to each other and themselves that severely limit how they are supposed and not supposed to be.

I remember discussing what it meant to be masculine with a ten-year-old boy. This summarizes the definition he felt compelled to meet: *To be a man, act mean. To be tough, show you don't care. To be strong, don't get beat.* His conclusion was: "When you're around other guys, you have to be a man."

Puberty can be scary because of the magnified vulnerabilities to teasing that were less of a concern in childhood. An early adolescent girl can be teased for her supposed sexual looseness as a young woman: "You look like a ho!" She can literally be demoralized. Or she can be teased about her unattractive appearance: "What a load!" An early adolescent boy can be feminized, teased for his supposed lack of masculinity as a young man: "You're girly!" Or he can be teased for not performing well in sports: "What a loser!"

Consider the adolescent boy who starts having erections and night ejaculations and worries that these spontaneous signs of sexual arousal will occur in public. Or consider the adolescent girl who starts wearing baggy clothes to conceal how her body is maturing so that her peers or the older students will not notice and socially respond. There is also the boy or girl who can't prevent an outbreak of pimples. No wonder young people this age feel like ideal targets for teasing. It's no fun being called "pizza face."

With the onset of puberty comes the tyranny of the physical ideal—being the perfect looking young woman and the perfect looking young man. Early adolescents love physical beauty, but they feel physical beauty will never love them. Everyone, no matter how blessed by appearance to approximate these ideals, feels insecure, inadequate, embarrassed, even ashamed about some part of their bodies that nobody else notices. "My ears stick out too far." "My hair's too thick (or too thin), too curly (or too straight.)" "My eyes don't match." "I hate my lips!" And parents wonder why it takes early adolescents so long to get ready to go out in public. The sense of scrutiny they imagine others will give their appearance is magnified by their insecurity, and the fear of being teased about one of these "defects" is terrifying. At this age, boys are just as painfully self-conscious and self-critical about their physical appearance as girls are. They all feel in some way "defective."

In addition, the adolescent's degree of physical maturity influences how people treat him or her. How old one looks sets other people's expectations of how old one should or will likely act. So the fourteen-year-old boy who wakes up each morning with manly stubble that needs shaving is given an undeserved reputation among some parents of female class-mates as a sexual deviant who should not be allowed around their daughters. Or the fully matured thirteen-year-old girl is given a reputation of being sexually active, which is equally undeserved. The rule in early adolescence seems to be that wherever insecurity arises, it shall be teased.

In general, *the less one fits into family, the more one has a need to fit in with friends*. The more they act put off by early adolescent changes in their changing son or daughter, the more parents push the young person into his or her community of peers for understanding and acceptance and a sense of belonging that is sorely lacking at home. The more dependent on peers one feels, the more vulnerable to teasing and other kinds of meanness one becomes. Conversely, the more secure the young person feels at home while growing into adolescence, the less vulnerable to teasing and put-downs he or she will feel at school.

Puberty isn't funny. When parents act amused by this new social dimension of their early adolescent's life, teasing the son or daughter about having a boyfriend or girlfriend, they are making light of what is seriously difficult. This is a mistake, because there is already so much teasing and gossip going on among young people about who likes whom, who is paired up, who is breaking up, and the reasons why. Puberty not only creates insecurity around one's changing appearance; it creates enormous social insecurity from the sexual expectations that must now be met. How are boy and girl, now young man and young woman, supposed to know how to approach, talk, flirt, date, and even express liking for each other? How is one supposed to know how to kiss?

And what about going to the first middle school dance? Should parents push their son or daughter to attend? No. Leave readiness for this social exposure up to the adolescents. At least if they don't go, nobody can tease them about who their new boyfriend or girlfriend is based on whom they danced with. Neither can anyone tease them because no one danced with them. Or nobody can tease them about their dancing technique. In one case, the parents picked up their son from his first middle school dance, and his dad, meaning to keep things light, asked, "How'd it go, lady-killer?" His son was silent all the way home. Because socializing with the other sex really complicates early adolescent life, parents need to tread lightly when this new vulnerability begins.

It is common for early adolescent girls to be more "interested in boys" than boys are "interested in girls" in middle school. Going with a boy is part of acting more womanly. Consequently, early adolescent girls tend to take more social initiative with male peers and tend to treat getting a boyfriend more seriously than boys treat getting a girlfriend. Having a boyfriend signifies how a girl is now more of a young woman and even confirms a certain social standing among her female peers. For many boys this age, however, having a girlfriend is of less importance, and it can often become more of a social game, even a joke. This is why a middle school break up that a boy orchestrates can be really hurtful to a girl who had part of her new womanly identity invested in the relationship. So too, competition for boys can become divisive among girls, particularly when a girl's best friend betrays her by stealing her boyfriend, who may think it's funny to play the two against each other. Thus, teasing her about the break up (I hear you got dumped!) can be really cruel.

Because girls tend to enter puberty earlier than boys, they often begin acting womanly toward boys before boys are ready to act manly toward them. For this brief period in early adolescence, girls can become the social aggressors. At this age, there is another kind of teasing that socially mature girls can inflict upon less mature boys. Usually over the phone or the Internet, it takes the form of "coming on" to boys with sexually suggestive communication with the intent to embarrass. For boys, it's hard to cut off this communication without appearing uninterested and unmanly, when in fact they feel sexually intimidated by the raw messages they get. "I'm a babe magnet," an eighth grader finally told his mother, explaining why he didn't want to answer the phone when one of those girls was calling. Conversation that feels fun and funny to the girls may feel uncomfortable and threatening to the boys as a consequence.

What can feel uncomfortable for girls is boys "hitting on" them with crude, sexually explicit words and looks to express newfound manliness. For girls, it's hard to turn away the male attention that they want to attract, but it's even harder to tolerate what feels threatening and aggressive. "The way he looks at me just creeps me out!"

During childhood, male-female contact was of little interest. Many girls never had a boy as a significant friend in elementary school. Many boys never had a girl as a significant friend during this time, either. As a result, what they know about each other is often based on what their own sex has to say about the other—stereotypes from the developmental sexism that they acquired through ignorance and lack of social contact. However, come early adolescence and puberty and the awakening to young manhood and young womanhood that begins, now males and females need each other to help fill out their new sexual definition. But how are they to know what their definition should be? Now a new potentiality for teasing opens up from the stereotypes that entertainment and other forms of media have relentlessly portrayed to powerful effect.

For want of a better definition in relationship to their male peers, young women may identify with the stereotype of sexual attractor by focusing on personal appearance. For want of a better definition in relationship to their female peers, young men may identify with the stereotype of sexual aggressor by focusing on powerful performance. As a result, young women thin themselves down and act suggestively, while young men build themselves up and act toughly. What allows young men and young women at this formative age to escape the dehumanizing stereotypes of each other as young men and young women who have been surreptitiously taught? First, girls and boys must get to know each other as friends. Girls who have boys as friends and boys who have girls as friends are less susceptible to social awkwardness with each other and thereby less susceptible to teasing about their "relationships."

The more inexperienced and insecure in these relationships young people are, the more they can be drawn to the stereotypes for definition, namely the swaggering young man and the provocative young girl. Such exaggerated definitions can become targets of teasing. Girls may make fun of a boy for acting like a big man, and boys may make fun of a girl for acting like a sexy woman. This is a tough age for the development of their sexual identities: One can be teased for acting too manly or womanly, and one can be teased for not acting manly or womanly enough. But whatever the cause for teasing, parents have a role in helping their son or daughter cope with mean teasing. This is a *coaching* role, helping the young person understand the choices and strategies he or she has to respond with, so that the least possible damage is done.

Coaching about Teasing

To begin coaching your son or daughter about mean teasing, emphasize how this behavior always reveals more about the teaser than the person being teased. It usually reflects two sources of insecurity in the teaser. First, it shows how teasers need to put someone down to bring themselves up, to make someone else feel worse about yourself to make themselves feel better about their shortcomings. Students who feel secure about themselves have little need to torment others. For students who feel insecure, however, teasing can provide temporary relief. In other words, the lower on the social ladder one is, the greater the pressure to torment someone further down can be. Teasing in this situation says, "I may have low social standing, but at least I'm not as low as you." For the person at the top of the social ladder, teasing can be how he or she maintains dominance over those below.

Second, teasers usually make fun of traits that they don't want associated with themselves. Teasing is often defensive in this way, attaching a negative characteristic to someone else before someone can attach it to them. Thus, the person who teases others about "messing up" is probably afraid of making mistakes or looking foolish. The person who teases about dress is probably afraid of not wearing the "right" clothes. The person who teases about what someone doesn't know is probably afraid of appearing ignorant. Teasing tells far more about the person teasing than it does about the person being teased. This is important information for the person teased to understand. The parent might explain, "I believe the reason why you get teased for being so full-bodied so young is because other girls envy your growth. They wish they had it for themselves and worry that they won't." For a daughter receiving mean teasing on a regular basis, parents need to listen, empathize, support, and strategize. If they can help empower her to successfully cope with this mistreatment, she will come out the stronger for it. This is why you should reserve intervening on her behalf as a last resort, only undertaken with her consent, because she might risk adversely affecting the independent social world in which she lives. Well-intended parents wanting to make conditions better can sometimes intervene and make the situation worse, like the angry parent who confronted her son's tormentor after school: "Stop the teasing and leave my son alone!" Unintentionally, she ended up fueling the fire. Now her son was teased for calling in his parents. It's hard for the parent to remember that her son, not her, is the one who has to live in the social world of school. Stir that world up with her intervention, and he is the one who has to deal with the waves she made.

Not Taking Teasing Personally

Young people also need to be told the difference between being a *target* of teasing and becoming a *victim* of teasing. A victim feels injured by teasing; but a target does not.

For example, years ago I was giving a talk about adolescence to a meeting of the Little People of America (dedicated to providing support to people of short stature and their families) and a mother told this story about her twelve-year-old son who was a dwarf. She described the day he came home from school and explained how he was teased about his short stature by some larger boys in class. As he described the fun they made of him, his mother listened and teared up. That's when her son asked, "Mom, why are you crying?" Then she explained how hurt and angry she felt at the mistreatment he was receiving. Whereupon, her son just smiled. Then he said, "Oh, Mom, don't cry. The teasing isn't about me. It's about them! It's just them wanting to be mean."

"So what do you do?" asked his mother.

"I just laugh and boast," he explained.

"Boast?" she asked.

"Sure," he replied. "I tell them I win, because nobody my age can be shorter than me! And they take their meanness somewhere else."

I never found out how this young man learned to master this vital distinction about teasing, but notice the two separations that he was able to make, both of which kept him from feeling like a victim during this verbal attack.

- Because he treated the teasing as being about the teasers and not himself, he did not take it personally, and so he felt no personal blame or shame.

- Because he exercised strength of social choice on his behalf, he did not feel powerless in response to being teased, and so he felt no helplessness.

As for his tormentors, I guess they found that it was no fun teasing someone who could laugh at himself (and was secretly laughing at them).

Victims feel helpless, because they feel that they have no choice. They need to know that they don't need to stop the teasing in order to stop the teasing from hurting. The two can be handled separately. To stop the teasing from hurting, they can simply stop taking it personally. Words intended to wound cannot hurt without the victims choosing to take the mean words to heart. They take teasing to heart when they treat the taunts as truth. As mentioned earlier, victims can re-member how teasing always tells much more about the teaser than the teased—how it expresses a desire to be mean and usually attacks a trait about which the teaser feels threatened and insecure.

An effective way for parents to empower their children who are being mean teased is to equip them with choices that tend to discourage teasing by giving the teaser unanticipated and unsatisfying responses. Consider just a few of the choices adolescents have when mean teasing comes their way:

- They can agree with it: "You're right. I sure dress strange sometimes."

- They can express interest: "Can you tell me more?"

- They can ask for repetition: "Could you say that again? I wasn't paying attention."

- They can pretend to misunderstand: "Oh, I thought you were talking about her."

- They can shrug it off and dismiss the insult: "Whatever!"

- They can act as if they don't understand the point. "So what?"

- They can ignore what was said and not respond: Give a blank stare and then walk away.

- They can declare they don't like being treated that way: "It really hurts when you say that to me."

- They can make fun of themselves and laugh along: "I sure am good at messing up!"

- They can tease back in kind: "Well, the same to you, too!"

- They can give a sarcastic response: "Thanks for the compliment!"

- They can call the teaser on the teasing: "Are you finished acting mean now?"

- They can bypass the teasing: "When you're done insulting me, let's do something fun."

The point is that they have choices, and the more choices they have, the more empowered they will feel, the less a helpless victim when teasing comes their way. That's the message the coaching parent has to give: "There is always something you can do, so if one choice doesn't seem to work, just try another. And remember, the responses that violate the teaser's predictions tend to have the most discouraging power."

Violating the Teaser's Prediction

To discourage a continuation of teasing, an adolescent can expand his or her set of responsive choices. One way to do this is to ask oneself two very powerful questions. First, the young person can ask, "How does the teaser predict I will respond?" Usually, teasers have an outcome in mind that they either think will happen or want to happen. For example, maybe one adolescent boy thinks the teaser's prediction and desire is that by making fun of his appearance he will become sad, silent, and socially withdrawn. In this case, the teasing has the intended effect of shutting him up or getting rid of his presence. Now, he asks himself the second powerful question. "In what ways could I violate the teaser's prediction?" In this case, the boy could choose to act happy instead of sad, speak up instead of shut up, and interact with the teaser's companions. So he just laughs along with the teasing, uses it to start humorous conversation, and socially sticks around. Now teasing has actually accomplished the opposite of what the teaser predicted or wanted. It has given the boy a way to join the group rather than be driven him away from it.

Your children are not responsible for being teased, but they are absolutely responsible for the teasing they do and how they respond to being teased. Of course, sensitive children are the most satisfying to tease, because they are so easily injured and can get so dramatically upset. Therefore, if you have a sensitive child who is often hurt (and many early adolescents fall into this category), you have to school him or her in how to avoid taking teasing insults to heart by treating taunts as truth or by treating the meanness as evidence that he or she has earned or deserved this mistreatment. If the child does take it to heart, he or she should at least learn how to avoid exposing the injury at the time. That emotional expression—crying or getting angry, for example—can make a young person the target of teasing in the future. When he or she acts upset, the victim only encourages the mean treatment to continue.

Teach your children the rule of *then and later*. Say, "See if you can take the teasing without expressing hurt right *then*, when you come home, tell us all about it *later*. We don't want you to deny your honest feelings, only to delay expressing them until it is safe and we can offer you support at home, and maybe some guidance for keeping the teasing down." Parents need to communicate that while they are advising their adolescent to act unaffected by mean teasing, they are also saying that the emotional effects of teasing should not be disregarded but expressed at a later time with them.

When Your Child Is Doing the Teasing

But what if your child is the one who is doing the mean teasing? Suppose your son laughingly describes making fun of another boy who easily cries. As a parent, you may want to correct your son's behavior so that it doesn't become ingrained and so that he can question the wisdom and ethics of his actions. You can explain to him some of the costs of engaging in mean teasing and other social cruelty. For example, you might itemize the damage done. When adolescents tease another student meanly:

- They treat themselves as a mean person.

- They deliberately hurt another human being.

- They are more likely to do so again for having done it before.

- They are modeling social meanness for others to follow.

- They are creating a social reputation as a mean person.

- They are putting others (even friends) on notice that you might treat them the same hurtful way.

- They are increasing the amount of meanness in their social world.

- They are encouraging meanness to come their way in response to acting mean.

- They may be making an enemy down the road.

The social habits that young people develop in their more socially independent world of early adolescence are formative. They carry forward, so the teaser can learn to become sarcastic, the gossiper can learn to become slanderous, and the bully can learn to become coercive. Parents need to monitor not only the social treatment their child receives but the treatment he or she gives as well.

It is always worthwhile for parents to try to bring out the empathetic and sensitive side in their child who may be mean teasing. Typically, parents do this by posing a role reversal. "How would you feel if it was you on the receiving end of the teasing you are giving? How would you feel if other guys groaned whenever you came their way?" Then give your own value reference about this behavior. "I wouldn't want other people treating you this way, and I don't want you doing it to others." When it comes to committing any social cruelty, parents need to explain their ethical frame of reference or else their early adolescent will think, like some of his or her peers, that inflicting mean teasing and other kinds of social harm is acceptable.

And what do you tell your child who was not involved in social cruelty but saw it happen? What responsibility does the innocent bystander have? If you believe, as some parents do, that "if you're not part of the solution, you're part of the problem," then you may weigh in on social responsibility, as did one mother to her son. "I'm glad you weren't being treated mean or acting mean, but I'm troubled that you just stood by when you could have at least spoken up or maybe stepped in to stop the meanness. By saying nothing and doing nothing, you acted like the meanness was okay."

Then there are those adults who mean tease students in middle school. There can be toxic teachers who manage students with intimidation, using public put-downs to embarrass a misbehaving student in front of peers who act nervously amused. In doing so, the sarcastic teacher not only earns the enmity of the humiliated student, but he or she scares the onlookers who fear that similar treatment will come to them. Even worse, teasing to intimidate, humiliate, and dominate is endorsed and encouraged by this adult example. Now the classroom has become emotionally unsafe. If your child continues to be the target of public put-downs by such teachers, you may need to confront the adults responsible. Declare your willingness to work with your child on any behavior that needs correcting, but state your refusal to accept any more humiliating treatment.

Parents also have a responsibility to keep their home free of "mean teasing." This is more complicated than it sounds, because they must monitor both the teasing that they themselves may do and the teasing that may occur between siblings.

Although most parents tease in friendly ways that convey value and affection, that playfulness may not translate once the child enters early adolescence and becomes too self-conscious, too self-critical, too insecure, and too serious for his or her own good. While the child may have previously had a strong tolerance for laughing at him or herself, the early adolescent generally does not.

Essentially, young people don't want to be treated like children anymore, and they don't want to be kidded by parents in the ways they used to enjoy. A son may have once liked how his parents used to tease him for physically growing so fast, but when they now take humor in the changes from puberty, it can feel deeply embarrassing. So when their son starts undergoing a growth spurt and becomes more physically uncoordinated (until he learns to manage his larger body), his parents joke at his new clumsiness and laugh. "Don't trip over yourself!"

But feeling out of control of his body is not funny to him. From his parents' teasing, he concludes he looks as foolish as he feels. That's why he acts angry and pulls away. In general, it really helps for parents to keep the contact with their early adolescent free of teasing. Young people get more than enough teasing from their peers. And if there is an older sibling in the family who knows how to tease so it really hurts, and often does to keep the younger in his or her place, parents need to intervene and stop the damage. Mean teasing at home only increases the early adolescent's vulnerability to either giving or being hurt by it at school. But parents can let it be known that there will be no mocking, put-downs, sarcasm, insults, or name calling in the family. As one parent described it, "Once our kids entered late elementary school, we made sure every-one understood that family needed to be a tease-free zone. They had enough of that torment going on at school. They didn't need any more at home. They needed relief."

■ ■ ■

But there is some meanness that can feel worse than teasing. Ask a group of early adolescents, as I have, which mistreat-ment they would rather receive, either being teased or being ignored, and the majority always votes for being teased. Why is that? The answer is, at least when they are being teased, people are treating them like they are worth paying attention to, even though the attention feels bad. But when people reject them, they engage in another extremely painful form of social cruelty, *exclusion*. They are refusing to take a student's presence into account. In the words of one seventh grader who felt he belonged nowhere, "At least when people tease you, you are noticed. When they ignore you, you're not even there." Teasing can make the victim feel like a person no one likes, but exclusion makes the victim feel like someone no one wants to know. The next chapter describes how exclusion works.

CHAPTER FOUR

EXCLUSION

Trish's family had just moved to town from a larger city, and so she was new to the eighth grade there. Very popular in her last school, she expected a warm reception at this new one as well. But she was mistaken, because the opposite experience occurred. Her winning ways were held against her. What she didn't understand was how her attractive presence would threaten the established order of the socially ruling girls. Unaware, she was providing fresh competition among traditionally popular girls for male interest, girls who were used to having the social field to themselves. Rather than welcome Trish and offer her friendship, the other popular girls did all they could to keep the interloper out. They didn't talk to Trish. They ignored her. They left her out. They let her know they didn't want her to join whenever they were hanging out. They treated her as an undesirable person, and so even the popular boys left her alone. It took Trish almost the entire fall to finally break through the wall of exclusion that had been erected against her. Her only crime had been that she was "new."

In Shakespeare's play, the elemental question may have been "to be or not to be," but in today's early adolescent culture, the most pressing question often is, "Are you in, or are you out?" Sally may get a boyfriend, but jealous girlfriends conspire to tell the boy lies about what Sally did with another guy. Believing (or wanting to believe what he was told), the boy ends the relationship with Sally. *Break ups* are powerful experiences of exclusion for the rejected person, not due to loss of romance so much as the loss of social standing and social identity. In middle school, having a boyfriend is more important for girls (who are more socially advanced at this age) than having a girl-friend is for boys. For a girl, having a boyfriend affirms one's young womanhood. Cruelest of all can be a double betrayal of the victim. "When my best friend stole my boyfriend was the worst time of my life. I didn't have him to go with, and I didn't have her to talk to, and everybody knew I'd been cut out! I don't know which was worse, not having them to talk to or having everybody talking about me!"

Exclusion is the act of rejecting someone who wants to es-tablish a relationship with you, denying them membership in your group, kicking them out of your group, or subjecting them to social shunning. It separates and isolates someone from the companionship that he or she wants or once had. Exclusion is how insiders create outsiders.

- By rejecting someone who wants a relationship, the excluder succeeds in making the other person feel inadequate. "I'm busy with my friends right now."

- By denying someone membership who wants to join, the excluders succeed in making the person feel unpopular. "We don't have any more room at our lunch table, so sit somewhere else."

- By shunning someone who wants acknowledgment or recognition, the excluders succeed in making the other person feel isolated and alone. "Act like they aren't even there."

In these cases, the excluder seeks to cut out, totally ignore, or disassociate from another person. The payoff for the excluder is the power to be socially selective, keep social competition down, and punish someone by keeping or turning them into an outsider.

■ ■ ■

Of course, nobody can claim membership in all student groups. Each group is exclusive to some degree, formally or informally deciding who belongs and who does not. This is particularly true of cliques and clubs and gangs—extremely tight-knit groups that exclude others to partly unify the people who are "in." At an age when many young people suffer from insecurity and lowered self-esteem from loss of childhood, exclusivity can establish social membership, social standing, and self-importance.

For the people rejected, it can hurt to have their application refused. Even more hurtful is when friends expel them from the group in which they had a place, turn against them, and then shun their company. Boys tend to experience exclusion as a loss of *companionship*, losing other boys to *do* activities with, being left out of the fun. Girls tend to experience exclusion as a loss of *intimacy*, losing other girls to *be* in close communication with, being cut out of the social know. Exclusion can happen in the real world, but it can also happen in the virtual one, especially when access to an online communication group of friends is suddenly denied. At that point, you are truly outside the loop. To exclude someone is a powerful act of social cruelty.

The Psychology of Exclusion

Already in a state of separation from family, the early adolescent is now particularly needful of peers—hence, the impact of social exclusion when it occurs.

To appreciate the power of exclusion in early adolescence, parents must understand the importance of *belonging* in children's lives. Belonging is equal parts *attachment* and *affiliation*.

- *Attachment* to parents provides the child with the primary dependency and trust that contribute to a sense of *personal* security.

- *Affiliation* with family provides the child with membership that contributes to a sense of *social* identity.

In most cases, early adolescence loosens the connection to family for more independent growth. Some degree of disconnection from parents at this juncture is normal. As the young person pulls away from his or her childhood definition and treatment, however, the adolescent can feel more distanced from family, blaming this distance on the difficult-to-live-with parents. Adolescents may even accuse their parents of not wanting them around when in actuality it is the young people who want to be less involved at home. Therefore, the early adolescent is much more sensitive to exclusion outside of family and needful of inclusion with peers than he or she was as a child.

In the best of possible circumstances, a growing child who develops adequate attachment and affiliation with family comes to feel positively connected to him or herself and confident about connecting with others out in the world. In this ideal childhood, there is comfort with the self and others through bonding with family. In the harshest of possible circumstances, the adolescent feels unattached and unsafe, disaffiliated and disconnected. In the latter childhood, there is a basic anxiety that creates insecurity with the self and others. Among more disconnected children, the need for attachment and affiliation with peers during early adolescence tends to be higher than for those children who were securely bonded with family. (Foster children moved from home to home, for example, may come to rely on friends for primary attachment and affiliation.)

One of the most powerful and common sources of family detachment and disaffiliation in early adolescents is the occurrence of parental divorce. This event weakens their attachment to parents. By breaking their commitment to the intact family, the parents have broken trust with the child. The lost marital connection between parents severs the home and tends to come at a bad time for the early adolescent who, in the process of separating from family for more independence, feels more disconnected from parents as well. Divorce loosens affiliation, because now the early adolescent, in addition to harboring grievances over the divorce, has less time with each parent, and even less when either remarries. Divorce also causes the young person to push harder for social independence with peers, because parents have now proved themselves more unreliable than they once seemed. Feeling more on their own, adolescent children of divorce become more committed to creating a social life apart from family. They tend to be more reliant on peers for attachment (trust and dependency) as well as affiliation (membership and identity). Remarriage tends to create even more disconnection from family for early adolescents than for younger children who are typically more open to bonding with a stepparent.

Whatever the state of family stability or change, however, the challenge for parents is twofold. First, they must accept the young person's need for less social companionship with them while they continue to invite contact so that their adolescent can still affiliate with them and feel part of the family. And second, through loving words and actions, they must affirm that the bond of their attachment is as strong as ever, despite more time apart and more frequent disagreements developing between them.

Well connected to parents and feeling like an active part of the family, the adolescent will be less vulnerable to significant injury from exclusion by peers, should it occur at all. The same cannot be said for young people who feel extremely disconnected and unattached to parents. These young people are more desperate for peer belonging and much more impacted by exclusion—when they can't get "in" or they have been kicked out. They are also more likely to use exclusion to make their social way through school. *The more unattached to parents and disaffiliated from family the early adolescent becomes, the more he or she will need compensatory belonging with peers—to confirm personal security, social membership, and adolescent identity.*

Secure attachment and affiliation with friends at this age becomes harder to attain, and the experience of exclusion becomes more common. Much more so than in childhood, peer relationships in early adolescence have become *politicized* by the quest for *group membership* and *popularity*. Group membership means one has a reliable social place with peers. Popularity means one has a high social standing based on the number of people who are and want to be one's friend. (By politicized, what I mean is what happens when young people start socially jockeying to secure or advance social position, both of which can be problematic.) Let's take a look at each in more detail.

Group Membership

For most young people, it would seem having a group of friends could only be a good thing. For middle schoolers, however, peer group membership is problematic because this new family circle of friends can be as confining as their relationship with their parents, only in a different way. Although there is no adult authority determining the terms of conduct, there are norms for the group membership that must be observed. These *norms* dictate that one must *conform to belong* to maintain good standing within the peer group. There are times when this requirement feels oppressive, when this tacit code of conduct means adolescents must do some of the following to be accepted:

- They must behave like them.

- They must believe like them.

- They must follow along with them.

- They must agree with them.

- They must not tell on them.

- They must dislike what and who the others dislike.

- They must appear like them.

- They must like them best.

- They must have no competing outside friends.

- They must not do better than them.

- They must defer to highers-up within the group.

Not only are these terms often the conditions for inclusion, but if they are violated, they may cause exclusion as well. There are many different ways that breaking these rules can cause exclusion. As one seventh grader explained her expulsion, "Because I started getting into horseback riding, some of the girls I hung around with decided I was changing; and when I made friends with another girl who liked it too, they kicked me out, saying I was trying to act better than them." *Asserting individuality can cause exclusion.*

Remember that peer group membership is not a free ride. It is not relaxing. It is not secure. It is a continually shifting network of relationships that can feel closer one day and more strained the next, as young people sometimes socially sabotage and scheme against one another while they vie for social position. This is why adolescents spend so much time talking, phoning, texting, emailing, and messaging each other. Staying current with your peer group so that you know what's going on takes constant attention and work.

Sometimes just standing out from the crowd can merit exclusion, as it did for the boy who had skipped a grade because he was academically advanced. No longer among the classmates his own age, now he entered into an older world where his comparative youth was held against him. As smart or smarter than the older boys, he wasn't as socially or physically mature, and they refused to associate with someone so young. No one would sit with him at lunch or socialize in class with him for most of the year. Less mature boys joined in the exclusion to avoid being excluded, too. *Being different can cause exclusion.*

Cell phones and computers have become essential electronic connections for social survival. Even then, it's hard to keep up in this fickle world of uncertain and shifting alliances. What you don't know can hurt you, as it did with the girl who didn't hear about a break up and asked the popular girl, who had lost status from losing the boyfriend, about the romance. The jilted girl thought she was being teased. Then, out of anger, she not only severed the relationship with her ignorant peer, but got other girls to take her side and join in the exclusion. Now, no one will sit with her at lunch. *Being uninformed can merit exclusion.*

Maintaining social inclusion, however, is not that simple, because there are hard compromises to be made. To gain group membership, adolescents give up individual freedom and sacrifice some personal honesty, as they sometimes feign enjoyment and appear to agree in order to be accepted. It's not only that peer groups insist on conformity; they can also deal harshly with nonconformity, even excluding a group member for violating the code of belonging by refusing to go along with an action or commitment. Then the group may punish the departure with gossip. The eighth grader explains how his world tipped upside down when he refused to join in the latest misadventure that excited his buddies: "Just because I refused to sneak out and go tagging, they kicked me out and then told everyone how I wasn't up to running with them. Now I don't have them as friends!" *Asserting independence can cause exclusion.*

Part of social independence is telling parents less about what is going on, or even lying to parents when things are going badly with friends by pretending all is going well. Although less truth is often told to parents during adolescence, young people do tend to be more honest with parents than peers on a very significant level. Adolescents feel freer to say what they like to parents, because parents will always love them. With peers, however, adolescents must often say what their friends like to hear, because these relationships are less committed. Basically, it's the difference between unconditional and conditional acceptance.

Thus, when angry parents say "You'd never talk to your friends this way!" to their outspoken adolescent, they don't appreciate the positive side of their complaint. It simply affirms how the young person feels safer to act unguarded around family than among fickle and less trustworthy friends. Summarizing the words of a thirteen-year-old, "I can pop off with my parents, but I have to watch my mouth with my friends." Usually, the early adolescent, no matter his or her degree of separation from parents, does not fear the exclusion from the family, though exclusion is always a threatening possibility with friends. *Saying something to peers without thinking can make an enemy and cause exclusion.*

One common experience of exclusion for many young people in early adolescence is the pulling away from old childhood friends who no longer socially fit into their way of thinking or behaving. This is a change that is cruelly felt but usually not cruelly intended. Changing interests and shifting cultural identifications reduce the old commonalities that they once shared, as early adolescent differentiation takes its toll on former friendships. As one young man described it, "When I became a skater and my old friends stuck to team sports, they stopped wanting to hang out together, and after a while so did I." For the friend who feels cast-off, the sense of loss can be profound, creating doubts about his or her worth and capacity to maintain a social hold. In this case, parents of the team sport students were implicated in the exclusion, because they didn't like how the skater friend dressed differently and suspected he would be a "bad influence." *Becoming different can cause exclusion.*

Most painful is when childhood friends *exclude* one of their own numbers to anchor themselves in the uncertain, emerging new social order of adolescence. The law of social survival can be harsh. Sometimes, it feels as if one must sacrifice others—even friends—to secure oneself in this emerging world of middle school relationships. As it was told to me, "Sometimes, to get new friends, you have to cut an old friend out." For adolescents who are excluded, those people they thought were their good friends suddenly want nothing to do with them, because they're not cool or popular enough, or somebody is mad at them, or they were cut out so that others could ally—and the excluded friends usually don't exactly know why. *Shifting social alliances can cause exclusion.*

Exclusion usually unifies the excluders and isolates the person excluded who feels cut out and cut off, even shunned. The cruelest part of this social cruelty is the lack of explanation that accompanies it. In the words of one hurt, scared, and bewildered eighth grader, "By myself is how I feel! How would you like to be frozen out? Be treated like poison? Not invited anymore? Given the silent treatment? Stared at and laughed at, knowing you're being whispered about? Never being spoken to? I thought these people were my friends!" Silence can hurt worse than words. Being ignored can hurt worse than being teased. What someone is not told can hurt worse than what he or she is told. More commonly an act of social cruelty committed by girls, sudden exclusion leaves the victim anxious and confused. They don't know what's going on. The excluded adolescents don't know what they did, and they don't know how to stop the exclusion. They feel very much alone.

Below are just a few of the many reasons exclusion occurs:

- Someone is angry with another and wants to get back at him or her.

- Someone wants to socially trade up by pushing another out.

- Someone wants to cut someone else out to make his or her way in.

- Someone wants to bring others down by losing their friends.

- Someone just likes having the power of expulsion.

- Someone, usually feeling bad about him or herself, wants to act mean.

- Someone would rather exclude another than risk his or her own exclusion.

- Someone joins the exclusion to show solidarity with the other excluders.

At worst, *boys may physically aggress* against one of their members to drive him out by pushing him around, while *girls may socially reject* one of their former members from their group. "Why didn't you invite me too? I thought you were my friends?" asks the girl excluded. One of the others dishonestly replies, "We didn't think you'd want to come along." *Exclusion can feel very cold.*

Unlike the other forms of social cruelty—teasing, bullying, rumoring, ganging up—exclusion attracts little adult notice at school because it is not socially disruptive. In fact, it is often invisible to the adults in charge. They don't hear the backbiting, nor do they notice the noninclusion, the noninviting, the hard looks, the freezing out, the crushing silences, the shunning, the secretive talking, the covert glances, and the group laughing that the person excluded is sure is all about him or her. Exclusion by whispering among girls is just as painful as exclusion by physical means among boys. In both cases, the person excluded feels disconnected and isolated. Worse yet, young people feel that exclusion is evidence of something wrong with them, and by keeping it secret, they can become further isolated, then making the secret a source of shame. Parents often only become aware of their son's or daughter's exclusion by noticing that the usual phone calls and invitations have stopped coming. "How come you don't talk on the phone to friends anymore?" they ignorantly ask.

As for those doing the excluding, they usually find excluding someone increases their own sense of inclusion, as they unify against the person being cast out. As one boy explained, "None of us hang out with him anymore." Like all acts of social cruelty, however, it is self-defeating to a certain degree, because it only demonstrates that what they do to others could be done to them. Any one of them could be excluded tomorrow just as their former friend was excluded today. As those committed to increasing their own sense of security had demonstrated, acts of social cruelty only make the larger social world that much more insecure.

What young people want is a guarantee against exclusion, so they pursue that Holy Grail of social security, namely *popularity*, only to find out how popularity itself is not secure at all. Popularity is like fashion. It is ever-changing with the shifts in current interests and tastes. In this sense, popularity is fickle and elusive. It is set by social forces larger than any individual can control.

Popularity

The gold standard for personal security is popularity. "In middle school, everyone is worried about popularity," I was told. "How do you know you are popular enough?" I asked. The answer I was given: "No one can be popular enough."

Popularity means adolescents have a well-connected social place among peers who want to be with them, with whom they have social standing and can hang out. Such characteristics as getting good grades, being intelligent, following rules, working hard, and being helpful to adults can all create a lot of popularity with teachers; however, such traits are unlikely to engender popularity with peers who place more value on looks, dress, possessions, coolness, hipness, athletics, and sociability. One interesting advantage of popularity can be the entertainment value of one's home. If there's a lot to do and a lot to eat at your home, with little parental supervision to get in the way, it can be a popular place to hang out. If the opposite conditions hold true, your son or daughter may prefer to hang out at the more popular homes of friends. For parents, the best compromise is accepting this attitude and welcoming friends without sacrificing standards of conduct one needs in the home.

At school, belonging is often signified by a certain gathering space, a physical place such as a hallway or courtyard at breaks or a table at lunch. "If you have nowhere to hang out, that means you have no gang of friends," it was explained to me.

Popularity is a measure of inclusion. If people are popular, they have lots of peers who include them, who want to be their friend. They have lots of company. If they are *un*popular, many people exclude them through ignoring. Few people want to be their friend. They must make their way alone.

Exclusion is a sign of unpopularity. This is why peers avoid association with an unpopular person. Exclusion puts the offending person at a social distance. Known by the company one keeps, befriending an unpopular person can increase one's risk of exclusion.

To be "picked on" can also mean that one is not popular. The less popular one is, the more one can be picked on—it's that simple. The more adolescents associate with people who are picked on, the more they put their popularity at risk. It's like unpopularity is contagious, and it can be caught through public association. Nobody wants anything to do with anyone who is so unpopular that he or she gets tormented all the time.

One girl explains why she no longer talks or sits by another: "I don't want to be seen with her and have other people get the wrong idea we're friends."

Conversely, the more popular people someone knows, the more likely he or she is to be included. As the same girl explained bluntly, "The best way to avoid being unpopular is to avoid having unpopular friends." And she nailed the truth, because popularity is based both on exclusion and inclusion. To be included in a popular group, you need to exclude and disassociate yourself from those whom the group does not want in their company.

It is here that parents can make an intervention by explaining what exclusionary social choices can cost. They can talk to their young person about the larger world that he or she will enter as an adult, a world filled with human diversity. In this more complex world, the capacity to get to know and get along with many different kinds of people will have a bearing on how well the adolescent makes his or her way in the future. Then they can explain how *now* is preparation for *later*. If adolescents shrink their social world as they grow through the middle school years by sticking to an exclusive group that excludes others, they will narrow their circle of acquaintances. In doing so, they will limit their social preparation for the larger, richer, more diverse world of life experience that lies ahead. It is a better social preparation in school to get to know students from many groups than only those restricted to his or her own. *Exclusion limits association.*

Any time young people exclude someone from their circle of acquaintanceships, they diminish their social experience and may lose the opportunity to get to know someone they might grow to like. The chief criterion for excluding someone is usually diversity (the person is "different from us"); the chief criterion for including someone is usually similarity (the person is "like us"). What the young person needs to know is that the more similar the people in his or her group, the more pressures to conform arise, and the less allowable diversity, the harder it becomes to express one's individuality, and the more limited one's social exposure becomes. This is why cliques and gangs are so powerfully oppressive. When the group dictates the definition of them all, inclusion becomes the enemy of individuality.

And being popular with one group isn't just enough, as there is the popularity ranking between groups. For example, the jocks are usually more socially prominent and powerful than the computer kids. The cheerleaders and the basketball players may be more socially prominent and popular than the drama students or the goths. I asked an eighth-grade boy why he was trying out for the team when he didn't have much interest in athletics, and his answer was completely practical: "Guys who play football are more popular." When it comes to popularity, sometimes people just have to do what they need to do.

And there is popularity within groups. Where in the pecking order does a member fall? What group one is in and one's social rank within that group are measures of how popular someone is.

Not only does a group not have room for everyone, within the group not everyone can be the leader. There are always leader wannabees, followers, and hangers on. A group is doubly powerful at adolescence, providing not just a social place but a social identity. By definition, if one is a member of good standing in an identifiable group, some degree of popularity is conferred simply as a function of belonging. If one is a member of a desirable and exclusive group, one's popularity can be enhanced. For example, the high social standing of cheerleaders is confirmed by the performance exposure that these competitively chosen few receive at athletic events. Exclusivity communicates that not everybody can get into the popular group.

Cliques and gangs are the most exclusive groups, because they are extremely selective and protective. Exclusion is a major dynamic that keeps cliques together by keeping others out. In this way, membership is limited to a chosen few. Members demand loyalty and shared identity, and they choose not to let "different" people into the group. Often members are easily identified by their common dress code (style, color, and look) that signifies belonging. Goths, for example, commonly dress in dramatic black clothing; goth girls often wear dark makeup and black fingernail polish, achieving a hollow look. Other cliques or gangs can emphasize designer clothes or show allegiance by wearing a certain color. Young people who gravitate toward cliques or gangs tend to be more disconnected from parents and in need of a social home—a place where they can belong and identify with others, a place where they can connect to other adolescents and feel accepted.

Cliques are protective because of loyalty and confining because of conformity. They usually have a clearly defined hierarchy of social rank. In general terms, there are three ranks, and each comes with a different kind of pressure.

At the top are the *leaders*, who enjoy dominance. But it takes a great deal of work to maintain their image, position, and influence. Female leaders have to take very good care of their appearance, and male leaders have to act tough enough so they don't take any "stuff" from anyone.

Next are the *aspirants*, those members who want to be leaders (or are leaders in waiting) and spend much of their time maneuvering and jockeying with rivals for the favor of those above.

And last—the lowest down—are the *attendants*, members whose role is to follow and act as audience for those in the higher ranks, as well as absorb (without complaint) any social meanness directed their way. One young man described how he was the butt of all the jokes in his clique of buddies, the person everyone could make fun of without fear of reprisal. "I'm the one everyone laughs at." What kept him accepting this thankless role? His fear of exclusion if he had objected. Better a thankless role than none at all. The smaller and tighter the group (like cliques), the greater the fear of exclusion most members harbor, because belonging is so important to them.

Sometimes, a person with just a few good friends actually has more friends than someone who has worked hard to gain popularity. Why? Because although popularity is often seen as the royal road to happiness, it can prove to be a source of more unhappiness than one anticipated. Someone who elects to keep just a few close friends and avoid joining any identifiable group— as an only child often will—truly likes (and is truly liked by) the company he or she keeps. Generally speaking, the same cannot be said of a young person who is part of a clique, gang, or other group in which only some members are close friends but others usually are not. As was explained to me, "Just because I hang out with all the jocks doesn't mean I'm tight with everyone."

To obtain and sustain popularity, there is a price to be paid. It is worth itemizing some of the common costs that come with being popular to young people in early adolescence:

- *Popularity takes striving.* They have to keep being nice to people whom they want to keep liking them.

- *Popularity takes staying current.* To stay popular they have to look cool and stay cutting edge.

- *Popularity is political.* People can vote them in, and they can vote them out.

- *Popularity is precarious.* It is hard to get, hard to maintain, and easy to lose.

- *Popularity is fleeting.* Like a fad, it can quickly fade when something (or someone) "better" comes along.

- *Popularity is partly unpopular.* While some people admire popular students , others may envy them, get jealous, and want to bring them down.

- *Popularity attracts detractors.* The more popular students are, the more people will gossip about them.

- *Popularity attracts imitators.* People act like popular peers so they can be liked by them and liked by others.

- *Popularity breeds insincerity.* The more popular people are, the more they have to fake being nice to others, and the more people fake being nice to them.

- *Popularity is confusing.* Sometimes popular adolescents wonder if people want to be their friend because of who they are or because they are popular.

- *Popularity brings attention.* The more popular people are, the more they are noticed, the more about them is judged, and the more closely their flaws and failings are observed.

- *Popularity is competitive.* Since so many people want to be popular, adolescents have to perform their best against their rivals every day.

- *Popularity can go to one's head.* Popular people can believe their own reviews and start to act special or entitled.

- *Popularity can be limiting.* The harder people strive for popularity at school, the more likely they are to invest less in creating a social life outside of school.

- *Popularity can be demeaning.* People who strongly desire to be popular will sometimes accept mistreatment from more popular people.

From what I have seen, those who experience the *least* social pressure from the possibility or reality of exclusion tend to be those who are neither the most nor least popular but somewhere in the middle. These young people often feel or possess the following qualities:

- They are content to have a few good friends.

- They are on comfortable terms with other students.

- They have other social circles besides the ones at school.

- They have outside interests and activities to enjoy.

- They have skills and competencies they want to develop.

- They have things to do to be a part of the family.

- They have ways to enjoy spending time with parents.

- They have ways to enjoy being by themselves alone.

- They have little hunger for the approval from peers.

- They have no particular ambition to be very popular.

If parents want to proof their early adolescent against being hurt by socially cruel exclusion, they should try to nourish these kinds of traits in their middle school age son or daughter. Central to all these traits is the young person's diversity of social choice that parents have supported by helping diversify the company the young person has learned to keep. Such parents encourage time alone, time with family, time with nonschool friends, and time with different friends from school.

What Parents Can Do

In a discouraged state, a young person who has failed to join the group he or she wants, or has been expelled from a group he or she likes, can conclude in their sorrow: "I'm so unpopular! This just shows nobody wants to be my friend!" No, it doesn't. Parents can help their adolescents gather the energy to socially reach out by shifting their focus from the few individuals who have refused them to many others they could meet. Help them list all the other people at school they might like to know, and even offer to host a gathering or outing to which they could invite new friends.

Few young people escape the pain of social exclusion growing through adolescence. The sense of loss, failure, rejection, loneliness, or isolation can really hurt. If parents see their son or daughter unable to shake any of these responses and get socially moving again, they may choose to intervene and help. There are several steps parents can take, including the following:

• You can provide transitional social company until other peer company is found.

- You can encourage positive ways for the young person to companion him or herself.

- You can use temporary lack of friends as an opportunity to develop new interests and relationships.

As one sad young person put it, "Hanging out with my parents is better than having no one to hang out with at all." During the course of this substitute companionship, there are some helpful statements parents can make:

- "Just because a few people don't welcome your company doesn't mean that there are not others who will."

- "Just because you feel they rejected your company is no good reason to reject yourself."

- "Just because you have given up approaching that group doesn't mean you should give up on approaching others."

For a young person who has been excluded from a "popular" group, parents can help clarify how popularity and friendship are not the same and should not be confused. Popularity is more fickle: comparative, competitive, and changeable. Friendship is more genuine: compatible, companionable, and constant.

"How can I tell if someone is really a friend?" Parents need to be able to answer that question for their early adolescent who can get so lost in the search and struggle for popularity that it's hard to know who's a real friend. To help, they can give the young person the four treatment questions he or she must be able to answer "yes" to for a healthy friendship to be affirmed:

- *"Do you like how the other person treats you in the relationship?"* For example, "yes" would be the answer if the person went along with what your son or daughter wanted as often as he or she went along with the friend. "No" would be the answer if the person was bossy and always had to have his or her way.

- *"Do you like how you treat the other person in the relationship?"* For example, "yes" would be the answer if your son or daughter felt comfortable honestly speaking his or her mind. "No" would be the answer if your child kept silent because he or she was afraid to disagree.

- *"Do you like how you treat yourself in the relationship?"* "Yes" would be the answer if your child felt he or she assumed equal standing. "No" would be the answer if he or she acted inferior in the relationship.

- *"Do you like how the other person treats him or herself in the relationship?"* "Yes" would be the answer when the other person can admit doing something wrong. "No" would be the answer if the other person blames him or herself when anything in the relationship goes wrong.

All "yes" answers would mean the young person has a friendship with significant value; all "no" answers would mean he or she has a friendship with much to change. A good friendship is one in which two people not only enjoy each other, but also enjoy the definition of themselves as friends.

Sometimes early adolescents will not see how their treatment of others explains the exclusion they are receiving. In this situation parents may need to gently point out the alienating behaviors that are resulting in people not liking their company. These antisocial traits often include being pushy, acting controlling, having a temper, acting bossy, being self-centered, acting sarcastic, or being extremely insensitive. They can also include acting shy, uncommunicative, and unresponsive. In these cases, there is complicity in one's own isolation, and parents need to suggest more engaging behaviors instead of alienating actions.

One dilemma faced in early adolescence is the conflict between pulling away from parents to establish more independence, companionship, and belonging with peers, and wanting to stay connected with family for security, nurturing, and love. It is easy for adolescents to act as if they want to be excluded from family membership, only caring about inclusion with friends. And it is easy for parents, put off by the more abrasive changes in their adolescent, to allow more exclusion from home and inclusion with peers. "All he wants is to be with friends and have nothing to do with family, and you know what? With the way he's been acting around here, sometimes that feels okay with us!"

But to let an early adolescent exclude parents and family from his or her life only reduces their influence and places more pressure on the young person to maintain inclusion and belonging with peers. *Feelings of exclusion from family only make the fear of exclusion from peers that much worse.* This is why parents, sometimes against their emotions at the moment and the outside pull of peers, must practice *inclusive parenting* during their son's or daughter's early adolescence. This means continually initiating contact and communication, recruiting him or her into family activities, and having their adolescent become an active contributor to the household and the family, all of which are directed toward linking the young person to family as he or she pulls away.

What was mentioned in the last chapter bears repeating here. If school is the only place in which a young person gets to interact with peers, then the injury will be amplified when relationships gets more unstable and hurtful, as usually happens during middle school, primarily because that is the only social world that counts. Parents need to make sure that their early adolescent is participating in multiple social circles so that there are additional opportunities for companionship outside of school, the major social venue for most young people. Just because an adolescent is being excluded at middle school doesn't mean he or she cannot be socially included elsewhere. For example, he or she can experience being included and valued as a member in the extended family, among neighborhood friends, on a sports team or club, in a church or volunteer group, or even in the company of good family friends. *Parents need to reduce their adolescent's urgency for and vulnerability to exclusion at school by creating multiple avenues of social inclusion outside of school.*

There's a measure of social security for the eighth grader who can declare, "I have lots of friends outside of school." A lot of these outside social groups (such as church youth groups) have much lower social pressure than cliques that dominate at school. If your adolescent explains how having friends and fitting in is "everything" that makes him or her feel good, then you need to understand that friends now matter too much. The most important and satisfying connection a young person needs to have is with him or herself, and part of the parent's job is supporting this primary relationship. Parents need to support their young children in learning how to keep themselves good company—being able to spend time with themselves and engaging in activities that cause them to feel good about themselves. Parents should want their adolescent to be able to not only happily socialize, but also stand happily alone.

The young people who can't stand being alone, who feel the company of friends provides the only context within which to grow, and who need popularity to feel personally affirmed are often most fearful of being excluded, most devastated when actually excluded, and most ruthless about excluding others.

There are several pieces of advice about exclusion parents might want to consider giving to their young person in middle school:

- "Don't try to join a group where you're not wanted. Look elsewhere to find your friends."

- "When you have been excluded by a group that didn't want you, or when you have been expelled from a group in which you belonged, don't reject yourself because you've been rejected. Appreciate yourself. It may be your injury, but it is their loss."

- "Any time you feel like excluding someone, just remember you are depriving yourself of getting to know someone you might enjoy."

Parents can be complicit in their early adolescent's exclusion. In fact, there are two common restrictions parents impose on their early adolescents as "good" reasons that can both increase their likelihood to experience exclusion by peers: *prohibiting entertainment* that is objectionable to the parents and *social grounding from contact with friends* as a punishment for wrongdoing. Let's start with the issue of objectionable entertainment.

Part of the parent's job is to determine what experiences to allow at this very impressionable age. They may feel a certain entertainment is too "adult" and then refuse permission for their son or daughter to see what they are angrily told by the young person "every one of my friends is allowed to see!" And he or she may be speaking the truth, because families differ in the cultural exposures they permit their adolescents to have. For parents, the issue is keeping their adolescent free from a disapproved influence, but the early adolescent still feels left out and excluded from an experience his or her friends have been able to share. This can be a tough call for parents. By keeping their son or daughter from the experience, they might end up partially excluding their child from his or her group of friends who are now all in the know. Ignorance of the majority experience can diminish social belonging. For parents, sometimes the best solution is a compromise. "We'll let you go on these conditions. We come along, although we sit separately from you and your friends. And later at home, we get to talk about the experience, discussing our impressions that we each came away with. We want a chance to hear what it meant to you and for you to hear what it meant to us."

Next, consider social grounding, a form of punishment some parents apply for committing a major (and sometimes minor) family infraction to discourage its repetition. They know social grounding is a particularly aversive consequence, because it limits freedom at an age when contact and company with friends feels important to their son or daughter. However, what they don't often know is the unintended consequence of taking their adolescent out of social play with friends, particularly if the grounding is for an extended period of time and not only prohibits association but communication as well.

Parents think all that is lost by this sanction is social companionship for a limited time, but they are wrong. The adolescent also loses up-to-date knowledge about what is going on among his or her group of friends, and the young person's absence creates an opening for someone else to assume his or her social position. When the grounding is over and the adolescent reenters the group, not only is he or she out of touch with the recent history of what has happened and lacking the experience others have shared, but he or she has been demoted as well. Taken out of play by social grounding, the adolescent has lost his or her previous social place. No wonder the young person feels left out and excluded, particularly if friends treat him or her as more of an outsider now. Feeling more insecure, more subject to peer pressure to conform, adolescents may or may not be able to recover their old standing in the group. For parents, this means that should you choose to use social grounding, keep it short and allow for communication with friends while your adolescent is serving his or her social time away.

Should you have a shy child, know that he or she risks exclusion for two reasons. Either his or her shyness will cause social timidity that keeps the young person from speaking up, joining in, and allowing other people to get to know him or her, or the adolescent's refusal to communicate and respond to social overtures will be interpreted as acting snobbish. As one girl explained, "The reason why we leave her out is because she acts like she wants nothing to with us." Acting shy can encourage exclusion.

To the shy adolescent who keeps getting hurt by exclusion, parents can say something like this: "There is nothing wrong with feeling shy. But there can be problems if you act shy, because by acting shy, you make feeling shy worse. So the trick is to gather your courage and act outgoing and responsive. The more you practice acting less shy, the more socially confident you will feel, the more other people will get to know you, the more friends you'll have a chance to make, the more included you will become. If you want to be included and make friends, you have to act friendly. Shy is not a friendly way to act. "

Then there were the parents of an early adolescent for whom exclusion mattered not at all, because being a happy loner preoccupied with many interests, he had no desire to be included. In fact, he saw social time interfering with his precious personal time to do what he loved. "Besides," commented his parents, "with all the meanness that goes on between kids at this age, middle school is not a bad time not to have a lot of friends." Students who are highly self-involved with their own interests; who have satisfying ways to enjoy their own company; who feel that having just a few good friends is company enough; have little desire for social inclusion; and being without a group to belong to poses no appreciable hardship. The happy loner mentioned above was a seventh grader who was caught up in his fascination with programming computers and his love for making music. He went through the middle school years pretty much out of the social swim and was very content that way.

As described in this chapter, exclusion hurts, because keeping someone out or kicking someone out of a group denies the early adolescent's need for social belonging. In the next chapter, I will discuss how bullying hurts in a different way, namely by creating a sense of danger or actually inflicting injury, both of which can inspire fear.

CHAPTER FIVE

BULLYING

"Where do you think you're going, creep?" asked the larger boy. This wasn't a question; it was a challenge.

"I'm going to class," answered Ahmed.

"Not down this hall, you're not," and then the larger boy pushed Ahmed back on his heels. "Go the long way around!"

"But I'll be late," said Ahmed, and then he was pushed harder, this time spilling some books on the floor that he scrambled to pick up.

Several more big kids came up and stood behind the other boy who was now clenching his fists. "Get out of here! Now!" Ahmed did as he was ordered. There were no teachers around to see.

Bullying is the poster tactic for social cruelty. It's the tactic that makes most of the headlines, because it represents how violently destructive social cruelty can be. It's the tactic about which over twenty state governments have written laws to prohibit it in the schools. *Bullying* is the use of hostile actions or words to intimidate, coerce, hurt, or appropriate someone who is usually weaker or more vulnerable.

- By *intimidating*, the bully succeeds in making the other person feel threatened and afraid. "I'm going to get you after school!"

- By *coercing*, the bully succeeds in forcing someone to act against what that person wants to do. "You'll do what I say!"

- By *hurting*, the bully succeeds in physically making the other person feel pain. "I said I'd show you, and I did!"

- By *appropriating*, the bully succeeds in taking or stealing what belongs to someone else. "Now what was yours is mine!"

In these cases, bullies seek to menace, get their way, or hurt another person. The payoff for the bully is achieving a sense of supremacy. Bullies bully those weaker to feel strong. For parents to help their child deal with bullying, they need to understand something about the psychology behind this behavior.

The Psychology of Bullying

In one form or another, all bullying satisfies a need for social dominance. But why does dominance at this age matter?

In early adolescence, establishing influence and maintaining social hold with peers are extremely important to counteract the insecurity rooted in the separation from childhood, the strained relationships with parents, and the challenge of social independence with peers. Feeling less "at home" at home, one's place and standing with peers becomes much more important. At this age, young people become more *insecure* within themselves, more *anxious* about the challenges ahead, and more *aggressive* about claiming independence. Bullying can compensate for insecurity, counteract anxiety, and become a social means for gaining control through aggression. For the bully, it can create a sense of being on top of the world, at least for a moment or two. For those bullied, the opposite is true. It can increase insecurity and anxiety, and it can testify to insufficient aggression to defend themselves.

It's important to understand that a bully is *not* simply a student who acts aggressively. There are many students this age who aggressively and routinely push more combatively against the adults and peers around them. *A bully is a particular kind of aggressive student—one who is looking for an easy victim and a safe target who will not retaliate.* Bullies exploit the vulnerabilities or weaknesses of others to feel strong.

The bully wants to assert dominance and control over someone who will quickly yield in submission or admit defeat. Some people say that bullies bully because they have low self-esteem; but that has not been my experience. For example, there was the young man who matter-of-factly declared, "I would rather be feared than be liked. I get more of what I want that way." At least they have higher self-esteem than the victims on whom they prey.

However, four common motivations for bullying are questionable:

- *To prove strength or toughness.* The problem is that people who have something to prove about themselves in order to feel accepted are by definition insecure. For example, the youngest of three brothers, forcibly kept in his place at home by the older two, was determined not to be at the bottom of the heap at middle school, so he pushed his way into prominence by doing to other students (who would take it) what his brothers did to him. People who feel confident have nothing to prove.

- *To defend and preserve social position.* The problem is that anyone who has something to protect feels threatened by others who might take it away. For example, the queen bee of her group in eighth grade keeps those below in line partly through her power of punishment. "Mostly, she's nice; but cross her, and you'll be sorry." People who feel secure have little need to protect.

- *To inflict pain in someone.* The problem is that people who need to hurt others are usually trying to manage or relieve some hurt of their own. For example, there was the seventh-grade girl whose parent had recently deserted the family. She regularly tormented a shy sixth grader all year.

Finally, the counselor got word of the bullying, confronted the older girl in her office, and got this explanation for what was going on: "I felt better making someone feel worse than me." People who are not in pain themselves have little incentive to cause pain in others.

- *To become popular.* The problem is that anyone who has to push people around to make a social place also alienates people in the process. For example, the seventh grader who could quickly wound opposition with sarcasm and scorn did achieve a certain social prominence, but because he was feared, not because he was liked. "He can really cut you down." People who "make" friends through intimidation have fewer friends than they think.

Just as people who tease reveal their own insecurities, the bully is self-revealing too, just in a different way. Because they believe in power, bullies respect power. This means they assert power to get respect; but they also are intimidated by power equal to or greater than their own. The fear that they exploit in others is one they usually harbor within themselves. This is why pushing back against a bully will often cause him or her to back off. Most bullies are only looking for a fight that they can easily win. They are not like the truly combative young people who love a good fight and go around challenging others to challenge themselves. Bullies want submission, not opposition; and they want it to increase their own strength of standing. Bullies are insecure this way. To keep their standing, they need others to give way or back down.

To Be a Bully

Particularly at the beginning of the school year, some bullies will troll the hallways for likely victims, verbally and physically pushing someone to test for signs of an easy mark. Bullies look for such signs as the following:

- Signs of *vulnerability*, like fearful looks

- Signs of *sensitivity*, like crying easily

- Signs of *insecurity*, like talking softly

- Signs of *avoidance*, like backing away

- Signs of *passivity*, like accepting mistreatment

Dominance, however, can have an unsuspected down-side—bullies can lack true friends. A fifth-grade teacher once demonstrated this to the classroom bully Zach, who was once again shoving other students as everyone got seated. Zach was always using his superior size to bump people in the halls and knock books out of their hands, because he thought it was fun and funny.

So the teacher used a nontraditional approach to deal with the classroom bullying. Although in this case it worked, it is not a method I'd generally recommend, because it is risky. It could backfire if the testimony that the teacher seeks is not given. This is what the teacher in our example did. First, she called Zach up to the front of the class, and in front of everyone, she asked: "Zach, do you have any friends?"

"Sure," he answered, "I have lots of friends."

"Like who?" the teacher asked.

"Like Ben and Shay and Danny," the boy answered.

Then the teacher said, "Let's see," and she called Ben up to join them. "Ben," she said, "I want you to do a very hard thing. I want you to tell the truth. I want you to truthfully answer me this question. Is Zach really your friend? Take your time."

After an awkward silence, Ben mumbled in a low voice, "No."

"Hey!" said Zach. "What do you mean? We hang out together. When I want to do something, you agree."

Then Ben spoke up. "That's just because you're bigger, and I go along to get along. It doesn't mean I like you as a friend. You're always pushing people around to get what you want!"

"Thank you for being honest, Ben," said the teacher. And then she repeated the same routine with Shay and Danny to the same end. Now it was just the teacher and Zach standing up alone, everybody quietly watching. "Maybe," said the teacher, "you need to treat people differently if what you really want is friends. Now you can go back to your seat." It takes a tough teacher to teach a hard lesson, and I'm not sure this intervention would have worked in middle school. She was confronting Zach with a couple of truths: A follower is not necessarily a friend, and bullies tend to have more followers than friends. Social dominance can come at a high social price. Most bullies are not as "popular" as they appear.

What some of Zach's "friends" may have been doing was "playing along." They went along with his bullying ways, acting as if he were playing, treating his behavior lightly, even laughing when that was not really how they felt. Zach may have been getting his way, but he wasn't getting honesty. He was getting pretense.

Standing Up to Bullies

One requirement for true friendship is that there be no fear between friends. A very popular seventh grader who abused the power of her position by bossing around those below discovered how the peers she considered friends were actually not her friends at all. One day, they collectively objected to her heavy social hand and cast her out. Partly in anger at her dominance and partly in anger at their own fearful submissiveness, they lead a revolt against her. They stopped being submissive and did together what none would have dared to do alone. They stood up for themselves. At the lunch table where they were gathered, the bully was throwing her weight around as usual, and on their prearranged signal, all the other girls got up and walked out, leaving the bossy girl alone only to boss herself.

Standing up to a bully can be scary and empowering, and sometimes it can have unintended consequences for the better. When a target of bullying doesn't back down, the bully is denied the dominance he or she seeks. Now the power difference between them has been diminished, and some mutual respect may have been established. The bully respects the other person, and the other person respects him or herself. Then, when the bullying stops, sometimes an unexpected friendship can develop as each discovers the other is a good person. In the words of one bully, "We had to fight to become friends."

Fighting

No question, bullying can lead to fights when the person being bullied decides to fight back. Parents come to the school for a teacher consultation about their sixth grader who regularly has been getting into fights. "He's very small for his age," they explain, "but he's gotten so combative! He retaliates very hard at the slightest offense, and he can be very provocative, often mouthing off to the larger boys. We've told him not to, but it's just no use." So what's going on? In many cases, early adolescent boys (and even girls) who are less than average size will develop their aggressive side to survive this rough-and-tumble age. They will launch attacks to cope with bullying that frequently comes their way. They fight to hold their social place. For parents, the fighting is seen as a problem, but what they don't see is the problem their child doesn't have—backing down to bullying, taking it without complaint.

There's more fighting in middle school than elementary school, because early adolescence is a more aggressive age than childhood. The goal of this aggression is to act more in control of what is happening in their socially independent world. As a result, young people learn to stand up for themselves, defend themselves, and assert themselves more aggressively. Consequently, middle schools have many more student fights to deal with than have elementary schools.

When someone cannot stand up to bullying or cannot find some way to stop the intimidation, significant damage can be done.

The Effects of Bullying

To understand the emotional issue of the victim, first start with a worst case scenario of the most extreme harm bullying might possibly cause. Remember the 1999 Columbine High School shootings—when, by all accounts, two badly bullied, counterculture students planted bombs and opened fire reputedly in revenge on the school for the mistreatment they received from the jocks. Although no one will ever know for sure the actual motivation that provoked this rampage because the two killers killed themselves, shame and rage may have been some of the combustible parts of the psychological grievance behind this act of violence. To a less dramatic degree, however, shame and rage are natural outcomes of being bullied.

Victims of bullying often receive a double dose of suffering, because in addition to being dominated and maybe injured, they become victims of shame. The victim of bullying can shame her or himself on a number of counts:

- Being selected as an easy target for attack

- Having some weakness to pick on

- Being pushed around

- Feeling frightened

- Not fighting back

Nothing destroys self-esteem as powerfully as shame. "Self-esteem" is two concepts compounded into one. "Self" is how a person *defines* him or herself. "Esteem" is how a person *evaluates* him or herself. Shame diminishes self-definition: "I am nothing but a victim." Shame makes a harsh self-evaluation: "I am worthless." The lower the self-esteem, the easier a young person is to bully; the more they are bullied, the lower their self-esteem sinks. This is a very destructive interaction, because it just builds on itself.

A parent's ongoing job, particularly during the insecure and vulnerable adolescent years, is to keep this cycle from getting started. Parents can encourage strong self-esteem by saying to the young person, "*Define yourself broadly and evaluate yourself kindly.*" Parents must continually respond to the whole person that they see and the positive characteristics that they appreciate so the young person can keep his or her self-esteem high. During the early adolescent passage when young people, ruled by a negative mind-set, are increasingly critical of their own physical and social image, parents must mirror a positive perception for their son or daughter to see.

A college student looking back on being bullied in middle school described it this way: "It's not the physical effects of being bullied that hurt most. It's the emotional ones, the ones that last. Being publicly bullied wears you down until you're nothing but a victim. It just eats away at you. You become a pushover in everyone's eyes, including your own. You don't like the bullies, but you dislike yourself even more. You're angry with them, but you're also angry with yourself. But what was a tall, stringy, funny-looking kid with thick glasses in middle school supposed to do? Turn the other cheek? Show how it hurts? Ignore it? Pretend it doesn't matter? Fight back and get hurt worse? Fight back and get in trouble with the school? Complain and get the bullies really angry for telling? Get tagged as helpless by asking for help? Where are the good choices? Come high school, I decided that was it. I wasn't going to take it anymore. And a couple times after school, I got into it pretty good. But finally standing up for myself changed my whole life. I showed myself I was worth fighting for even when I lost the fight. I got my confidence back... and my respect. No more disgrace, though I was still angry at being picked on. After that, the bullies left me alone. I guess I was more trouble to mess with than they wanted. A friend of my dad's who had been bullied understood. 'Better to deal with bullying with a blaze of courage,' he said, 'than to bear it like a cross of shame.'" Fighting back against a bully was how the young man fought to restore his sense of pride. As he fought and overcame his fear, he also diminished his sense of shame.

This connection between fear and shame is important to understand. Bullies do not create fear in victims; victims create that fear themselves, namely by believing they are in danger of getting hurt, which they well may be. What bullies are good at, however, is sensing and playing on those fears to manipulate the victims. A skilled bully can "see fear" in the other person's eyes. The sequence that leads from fear to shame is roughly as follows:

- Bullies exploit the victim's fear.

- Fear encourages the victim's helplessness.

- Helplessness yields to submission.

- Submission causes humiliation.

- Humiliation creates self-loathing.

- Self-loathing engenders shame.

- And in the worst situations, shame can lead to self-harm (what has been termed "bullycide," a suicide attributed to being bullied and suffering depression).

So bullying is serious business. Reports of a student suicide attributed to bullying testify to how the victim's emotional burden sometimes becomes too much to bear. For many adolescents, while it can be threatening to live in fear, it can be crushing to live with shame.

One school counselor I talked to years ago practiced what she called "victim prevention." She would go into classrooms and talk to students about bullying. She would first confront anyone playing the bully role by declaring how it was against school rules to act in any way that caused other students to feel unsafe. Then she would shift her focus to anyone playing the victim role. She talked about not playing what she called "give away" with a bully. She talked about the "bully game," as she called it, where the bully wins by taking power from the person being bullied to strengthen him or herself. "So," she advised, "if you don't want to be bullied, don't give away any kind of power. How should you react? Answer yourself this question: 'If I were to hold on to all my power of self-determination, how would I choose to respond?' Then, consider doing that."

This is not to say that the way to stop all bullying is to put the responsibility on the person bullied to stand up for him or herself. This could lead to blaming the victim by blaming the act of bullying on the person being bullied. Bullies must be held accountable, and they increasingly are, as more state laws and school safety policies are starting to send the message that bullying will not be tolerated. When bullying is ongoing or leads to assault, outside authority must step in. When a bully punches another student in the face as they pass in the hall, it can become a matter for the local police. And when bullying is ongoing, many school districts have policies that not only sanction the bully but also have victim services counseling and even allow the bullied student to transfer to another school. What the victim of ongoing bullying needs to understand is that reporting mistreatment to the school authorities is a responsibility because behaviors that threaten or injure one student endanger the safety of all.

What Parents Can Do

Perhaps the first job of parents when their son or daughter enters middle school is to assess the young person's susceptibility to bullying. This can be done by reviewing common combinations of characteristics that are often apparent in a bullying relationship to approximate to what degree their early adolescent is likely to take on either the bully or victim role. Start by reviewing the characteristics of each role, and then determine to what degree your child fits into either category.

BULLY:		VICTIM:
Older	vs	Younger
Bigger	vs	Smaller
Stronger	vs	Weaker
Confident	vs	Anxious
Bold	vs	Timid
Tough	vs	Sensitive
Loud	vs	Quiet
Social	vs	Shy
Outspoken	vs	Untalkative
Confrontive	vs	Avoidant
Aggressive	vs	Submissive

If, in your judgment, your son or daughter possesses many of the characteristics on one side or the other, you may have a bully-prone or victim-prone child. In both cases, talking to them is important in order to face the issue before it gets too serious.

Suppose, however, that your child is being bullied, but because the adolescent fears reprisal and feels some shame, he or she doesn't want to tell you about the incidents. How else can you know? The answer is to look for telltale signs. For example, the child may exhibit some of the following behaviors:

- One may act nervous and tense before school.

- One may appear to be suffering unusual fatigue from stress.

- One may get phone calls, just listen, and afterwards look upset.

- One may get text messages, IMs, or emails and afterwards look upset.

- One may complain about aches, pains, and not feeling well and want to stay home.

- One may be hard to get up in the morning and reluctant to go to school.

- One may be less able to concentrate and complete school-work, and his or her performance may drop.

- One may seem more sad and fearful and angry.

- One may talk about not liking school.

- One may want to be driven to school and dropped off at a certain entrance and time.

- One may be missing belongings taken to school or bringing them home damaged.

- One may come home with clothes roughed up or torn.

- One may need more money to take to school.

- One may show bruises, scrapes, or cuts that can't be explained.

Parents need to remember this is the age of social independence, when young people tend to become less commu-
nicative anyway as a function of wanting more privacy and
less scrutiny from parental oversight. In addition, as newly
minted adolescents, young people believe they should be able
to manage their relationships by themselves, without parental assistance or support. As a result, if they are experiencing
some social cruelty like bullying, they think that they should
keep it to themselves on principle of independence.

In good faith, parents will routinely ask their early adolescent in the evening, "How was your school day?" This is *not* a
good question to ask, because a mumbled "okay" or a shrug is
the best answer you'll get, and it is not answer enough. Parents
need to know more about what's happening in their child's
life, particularly if mistreatment is being received. They need
specifics, not generalities. And they need to be aware of how
unproductive these simple questions can be. Questions can
actually shut their early adolescent down, because they are
emblematic of the authority that the young person is resisting
and the invasion of privacy against which the young person
is protecting.

Parents are better served not by asking a question but by
making a request. Requests respect the right of the young
person to disclose anything he or she wants. "Can you tell me
a couple good things and couple hard things about your day?"
And before making that request, they are better off priming

the pump of self-disclosure by describing some good and hard moments about their day first. Parents who don't share about themselves are not likely to encourage personal sharing from their early adolescent. Sharing the experience of being bullied with their parents is hard for young people, so not only do parents need to elicit the information respectfully, but they need to respond without overreacting. The last thing a frightened, humiliated, or hurt child who is the victim of bullying needs is a parent who is emotionally upset and threatens to take drastic measures to make things right.

When Your Child Is Being Bullied

Of course, when they are finally told about how their child is being bullied, most parents get angry and feel protective. This is an understandable response, but for useful dialogue to continue, they need to emotionally restrain themselves for the time being. When a child becomes a victim of social cruelty, parents can feel victimized as well, primarily because they are dearly connected to their son or daughter. This is a warning sign.

When your child becomes the victim of bullying or other social cruelty, parents then need to provide empathy and support, but they should not cross the line and take the mistreatment personally acting as if they themselves have been mistreated. The social cruelty is being done to their child, not to them, and they must keep that separation clear. Otherwise, by acting as if they have become the target of the hostility, they will only serve to amplify the damage, confuse the situation, and compound the problem. *Their child needs them as an adult support, not as a fellow victim.*

In order to protect their child, they want to punish the perpetrator or at least contact some powers that can stop the bullying. This is when approaching the bully's parents comes to mind. For this to result in cooperation by the bully's parents, the parents of the student bullied have to be extremely tactful and sensitive. The victim's parents must act in a nonaccusatory and uncritical way, express concern for the welfare of all parties, describe the situation objectively and specifically, and ask for help on their child's behalf, not demand punishment for the other child.

Attack the problem by attacking the parents, and a defensive response is likely to be provoked—the parents of the bully will likely mount a defense of themselves and their child. I witnessed this response years ago when conducting a workshop on social cruelty for the parents of seventh graders. An outraged mother publicly confronted another parent about the bullying of her own daughter. The parent of the bully defended the accused child by blaming the victim. "My daughter is not a bully! Your daughter is just oversensitive. Kids will be kids. My daughter wasn't bullying yours. Your daughter won't stand up for herself. That's the problem!" Starting a fight between the parents does not ease tensions between the children.

Responsibility for Bullying Must Be Shared

Plus, the mother of the bully actually did have a point.

Consider a question to which your child needs to know the answer: How can you bully someone who won't back down? The answer is you can't. *There is no such thing as a self-made bully.* Bullies take what they are allowed to get away with. It is fear that encourages the bullied person to submit. To confront the bully, the young person has to resist his or her own fear, and this takes courage.

One of the reasons a young person won't tell parents about being bullied is because, thinking less of him or herself for being repeatedly pushed around, the adolescent is afraid the parents might think less of him or her as well. This is shame's work. Shame isolates a young person by keeping him or her quiet about what is actually happening to keep secret the worthlessness he or she feels. Parents need to tell their child that there is no shame in feeling frightened when it comes to being bullied, and there is no shame in yielding to threats, only *regret*. When the adolescent feels worthless, this only adds a self-punishment to the social punishment of being bullied, and it encourages giving up, because now one's well-being is not worth protecting. When people don't stand up for themselves out of fear, they usually look back on the incident with regret, because they wish they had acted differently.

However, standing up for oneself and speaking up for oneself when frightened is something nobody does all the time. In fact, it is the work of a lifetime. Here it helps if parents can describe a situation in their own lives where they allowed fear and threats to dictate their behavior. So the mother says to her daughter, "Just last week at work, I let a loud coworker shut me up. She knew I was afraid our disagreement would make an unpleasant scene, and she wasn't. Now I wish I could take that decision back. Having successfully bullied me once, she'll probably look for another chance to do it again." The parental message given here is instructive on multiple levels:

- "As your parent, I've been bullied too."

- "No matter how old you get, there will still be bullies."

- "How you deal with bullies now will affect how you deal with others later on."

- "What you let bullies get away with now, they are more likely to try with you again."

- "At the very least when you allow yourself to be bullied you end up with regret."

By openly discussing bullying, parents can reduce the likelihood of another damage that fear can cause: It can isolate by secrecy. Now being bullied becomes something he or she *should* talk about instead of something the young person shouldn't. Tell your child, "Should you ever feel frightened by threats or actions at school, please talk with us about it." Feeling bullied is not a good time to also feel alone. In addition, explain how when your son or daughter evades the person he or she fears— choosing a different entrance into school to avoid where the bully hangs out, for example—running from the source of his or her fear makes the fear that much more powerful. Thus, skipping school today because he or she doesn't "feel well" to avoid encountering the threatening experience provides temporary relief that only increases fear of the bully.

Appreciating Fear

Because they prey on it, bullies have much to teach the bullied about fear. It's not the bully but *fear* of the bully that gives bullying its influential power. And fear can build upon itself and injure the victims in multiple ways:

- They can feel afraid of the bully.

- They can feel afraid to confront the bully.

- They can feel afraid to tell people they are afraid.

- They can feel frightened into acting more afraid.

- They can let fear exaggerate the threat posed by the bully.

The end result may be that the people bullied bully themselves with their own fear, only increasing the power of the actual bully. So I counsel parents that they have three levels of help to provide their children. First, they need to open up a discussion of fear, and the best way is to share some of their own experiences with fear. Second, they need to talk about the management of fear, "How to let reason, not emotion prevail. Ask, how realistic is the worst likelihood I fear?" And third, they need to talk about how to deal with the bully and possible strategies that may include parents becoming directly involved with the school.

About fear itself, parents need to let the young person know that fear is nothing to be ashamed about. It is an important emotion. Fear is a natural response to real or perceived danger. Fear provides a warning. Parents can say, "Fear tells us to watch out, because we might get hurt, so fear tells you that this bully could do you harm." They can also explain how growing out of childhood and entering into the larger and more complicated world of adolescence normally increases the fears of most young people. There is simply more to watch out for. (Consider the dark poetry and violent drawings many young people do at this age, all authored by fear.) Finally, parents can share fears that they may have had growing up to let the young person know how adults who may appear to feel so confident now used to have many fears back then. They can say, "I was afraid people wouldn't like me. I was afraid I wouldn't have any friends. I was afraid people would pick on me. Middle school can be hard those ways."

If parents can recall their own encounters with bullies and how they handled the aggression, then that could be good information to share. One dad remembered, "I got really good at wordplay, verbally sparing with aggressive students to show that I could give it back, and that if I wanted, I could ignore threats and insults and let them go. Almost all the bullying I received started with words, so if I responded word-for-word, things rarely got physical. Also, I found it always worth testing the bully with some resistance, because then I brought some pushing back to the situation. I felt stronger, and a lot of times, what really happened was much less than what I feared would happen."

Sometimes an older sibling can be helpful, such as the one who explained his strategy for surviving middle school to his younger brother: "Get yourself some slack. Some backup. Get to know some of the tougher kids in your classes. Be friendly with them, even be of help. When bullies know who you're connected with, they won't mess with you. At least they never did with me." Another student described some harder support provided by his older brother: "I came home crying after school, because this big kid had thrown me to the ground and trashed my backpack. That's when my brother really lit into me, harder than what I feared the bully would do. Then he stood over me. 'Don't you ever come home whipped by anyone, you hear?' he said. 'From now on, you take care of business!' And I did."

Next parents can talk about the management of fear, particularly how letting fear take over can make bullying worse.

They can explain how by acting frightened, the young person can encourage the bully to continue, because the outward signs of fear is exactly what the bully is looking for. They can talk about how running away from the bully can increase one's fear. They can describe how listening to fear will exaggerate the danger by making the bully seem more threatening, often more so than he or she actually is. Then they can express respect for the young person's courage—the courage it takes to go to school where maybe bullying awaits. They can also identify another act of courage the young person has made—talking to parents instead of hiding from them. When the young person tells parents about the bullying, he or she breaks the isolation, receives some support, and ceases to protect the bully by keeping silent about what's actually happening. Now, they can add their coaching to the young person's courage to help him or her cope with the situation.

Dealing with a Bully

The more a victim of bullying a young person feels he or she is, the less choice the adolescent believes he or she has to stop the violence and fear. One role of the parents is to help their adolescents identify choices for dealing with the threatening or hurtful situation so they feel that they have some power to counteract what's happening. This is where more coaching is needed—helping the young person develop strategies and identify choices for dealing with the bullying.

The rules of conduct they may want to recommend can include approaching the bully as opposed to avoiding him or her, as well as speaking up to him or her instead of shutting up, so the young person can take the social initiative. One feels stronger being active than reactive. One can also feel stronger by having a plan. A very important part of that plan is how to posture oneself when talking to a bully. Posturing advice from parents can make a distinction between acting like a "victor" and acting like a "victim." (A school principal gave this distinction between victor and victim to me that she used to coach bullied students.) The distinctions she drew were the following:

A Victor:	A Victim:
Stands straight...	Slouches over...
Plants both feet...	Shifts foot to foot...
Faces the bully...	Turns to the side...
Squares shoulders...	Slumps shoulders...
Loosens arms...	Stiffens arms...
Raises chin...	Lowers chin...
Makes direct eye contact...	Avoids eye contact...
Keeps fingers lose...	Keeps fingers clenched...
Moves close...	Backs away...
Speaks clearly...	Speaks faintly...
Looks relaxed...	Looks nervous...

In confronting a bully, the nonverbal message counts for a lot. The young person can even rehearse this posturing with you to practice beforehand. Appearance can speak more strongly than words. In addition, how one acts affects how one feels, so if the young person acts (and it can be only an act) physically self-assured, not only will this assurance be conveyed, but he or she will experience some of that assurance as well. The role the adolescent fakes at first becomes the role he or she gradually takes. As stated earlier, it's when a student exhibits vulnerability, sensitivity, insecurity, avoidance, or passivity that he or she can leave "blood in the water" to attract the social sharks (bullies).

The job of the parental coach is to encourage their bullied adolescent to identify and pursue positive possibilities that will strengthen him or her as the young person faces the intimidator down. That said, the parent's job is also to help strengthen the young person in at least five possible ways:

- By helping the adolescent make more friends at school, the young person builds social support.

- By helping the adolescent build friendships in social circles outside of school, the young person builds a larger social world.

- By enrolling the adolescent in confidence building activities, the young person strengthens sense of competence.

- By respecting the adolescent's fear and the courage it takes to deal with fear, the young person builds self-respect.

- By giving the adolescent strategies for coping with the bully, the young person builds resourcefulness.

As for coping, there are two empowering questions adolescents can ask themselves: 1) "What would I choose to say or do if I were not afraid?" and 2) "What does the bully expect I will say or do, and how can I violate that expectation?" The answers to the first question will suggest some statements or acts of assertiveness that the adolescent has not made. For example, "Next time you pop me, I'm going to pop you harder back." The answers to the second question will suggest some statements or actions that will surprise the bully. For example, the last thing the bully expects is a social invitation: "Some of us are going to a movie and pizza this Friday. If you want to come along, let me know." Both statements have the power of social initiative.

One dilemma for parents and students when dealing with a bully is whether or not to encourage and engage in fighting back, which is usually against school rules. Besides, settling differences through physical conflict may not be what parents want to condone. What may be useful for parents to remember is this: Most physical bullies are action people who are out for an easy win, not a hard struggle. They believe in wielding the power of physical force to threaten and prevail, but they are not eager for a fight. They are looking for submission. When equal or greater physical force comes from the intended victims, bullies will often back down or at least act disinterested to save face. This suggests that sometimes supporting fighting back (if that is what your son or daughter wants or is willing to do) can bring bullying to a quick end. Should you choose to give this support, make it clear that you are not endorsing fighting in general, that you understand that the school may apply consequences for fighting, and that you will not punish your son or daughter for breaking the rules at school in this one instance.

Parents may want to give a double message: "The school will punish you for fighting, and we don't want you to get into fights. They don't want violence at school, and in general, we agree. However, if your words have not backed the bullying off and you choose to physically defend yourself, you will get into no trouble with us, even though you may pay for the trouble at school. The main thing is to get the bullying to stop."

A story about fighting back against a bully comes to mind. It occurred at a week-long summer day camp when a sixth grader started routinely intimidating a larger boy, Tim, who would become very frightened when exaggerated threats to him were made. "I'm going to hit you so hard I'm going to knock your heart up into your mouth!" And Tim would get wide-eyed and sometimes even cry. Toward the end of the week, a counselor who had observed this repeated bullying took the sixth grader aside and asked him if he would like to box with Tim, which of course the sixth grader thought was a great idea and readily agreed. Nothing like an easy win to boost superiority. In the makeshift ring, each boy, now wearing boxing gloves, waited to begin. The sixth grader was excited to get started, and Tim looked really scared. The whistle blew (there was no bell), and the fight began, but not how the sixth grader expected. Empowered by fear turned into panic, Tim (probably coached by the counselor) came out with both arms flailing, swinging like a windmill, and the sixth grader was quickly pummeled to the ground. Match over, and a number of lessons learned. Tim learned that by standing up for himself and braving his fear, he could face down a bully. And the sixth grader—what did he learn? Well, the sixth grader learned a lot. He learned to respect Tim and the courage it must have taken for him to put on those gloves. He learned how small it felt to be a big bully. He didn't feel proud of himself at all for trying to threaten and scare another person. And he learned that pushing people around was a lot less fun when they started pushing back. And he learned not to bully anymore. And in case you're wondering, that sixth grader was me.

Sometimes parents will deliberately enroll an early adolescent, particularly a boy, in conditioning, weight training, and sports competitions to help build confidence in dealing with physically aggressive behavior from peers, which can help. Martial arts and contact sports give young people practice with physical encounters that can prepare them for the increased push-and-shove behavior that comes during the middle school years.

If your child cannot stop repeated bullying, then he or she must get outside adult help. Repeated bullying must be stopped, because the more it is allowed to continue, the longer it will continue and the more extensive the damage done will be. The person bullied feels more helpless, worthless, and resigned. He or she builds a social reputation as an easy and deserving victim. The bully feels freer to continue the persecution, while others may feel pressured or encouraged to join in the "fun."

With the young person's permission, parents can approach the authorities at school. Suppose on the bus each morning your child is harassed by an older girl who demands your daughter's seat wherever she sits, spills her backpack into the aisle, and calls her demeaning names. According to the bus driver, your daughter is the troublemaker, indicated by the lack of problems on the bus before she is picked up. Feeling upset on your daughter's behalf is natural, but getting angry with the school principal or assistant principal will likely undermine your cause by putting them on the defensive when what you really want is their collaboration.

Concerned, reasoned, and specific is how you need to be. Your concern is for the well-being of your child. Your reasoning is that every child should have safe transport to and from school. And you bring a record of specifics describing times, incidents, players, and mistreatment to be discussed. You are going through channels—first, the school administration; then the central office; then the school board; and to the police if need be. You insist on safe passage for your child. If your child cannot bring bullying to a stop by standing up to the bully, parents should assume an advocacy role. Because in many states bullying is now against the law, there may be legal grounds for parents to use to compel the school to protect their child. They may even be able to get a restraining order against the bully that puts both the school and the bully's parents on formal notice. Sometimes, parents of the bully act ignorant of what is going on, not out of denial or defensiveness but because they really don't know. The bully has been successful at concealing his or her behavior from them. Formal action brings the bullying to everyone's attention.

Of course, with the advent of the cell phone and Internet technology, much bullying between students is no longer done face-to-face. It can even be done in hiding. People who wouldn't dare bully face-to-face now have another way. In fact, there is a lot of electronic bullying with texting and Internet communication (sending threatening comments or sexual requests in text or online messages, for example). There is even electronic stalking when unrelenting messages of a demeaning or threatening kind are so frequently sent that the victim feels as if there is no escape from this constant pursuit.

As for what to do when your early adolescent receives a bullying threat, a threatening request, or slander via texting, email, or messaging: send a *cease and desist statement*. Parents can usually stop this activity by joining the conversation. "Stop this messaging at once. Just because you are invisible, that doesn't make you untraceable. You have given us data to proceed against you. Know that you are now dealing with the parents of _____." If your adolescent is challenged at school for reporting the incident to you, your son or daughter can explain, "My parents monitor all my communication, coming in and going out."

Sometimes feeling bullied is experienced when no actual bullying is going on. That is, a young person can feel pushed around by someone acting dominant who doesn't mean to come off as threatening. So another job for parents becomes making sure that their child is not creating a bully where no bullying is present. For example, when their middle school daughter describes how her new friend Lillian can sometimes be a bully, parents may agree how she is certainly a challenging friend to have: "She does sound like she can get frustrated, even demanding sometimes, when she doesn't get her way. But based on our observations, she may not be a bully. Sometimes there are people who are just pushy, take charge kind of people who will run over you if you let them. They don't mean to bully. They are just naturally aggressive. That's how we think Lillian is. She's one of those people who are strongly spoken, who says what she thinks, and goes after what she wants. So if you're shy or timid or passive or quiet around such an aggressive person, she may run over you. She doesn't mean to bully. She just wants her way. What it will take from you is a firm, determined message to stop her charge." And so with Lillian, their daughter got to develop more of her assertive side. In their judgment, this is for the good because their daughter hasn't always found it easy to speak up and stand up for herself.

When There's Bullying at Home

But what happens if bullying is rooted in the family with a parent or an older sibling who intimidates, coerces, or injures for the sake of dominance? It happens. Growing up in this circumstance, there are two accommodations a child can make, both of which can encourage bullying behavior at school. A child can *identify* with the bully and model with peers what he has learned at home; or he can *adjust* to the bullying and take mistreatment from peers as he has learned to do in the family. In both cases, the formative lessons learned can create problems with peers. That's why you should confront the source of family bullying yourself, explain why it must stop, and keep your home bully-free. Many bullies learned to become bullies by being bullied themselves.

When Your Child Is the Bully

What should parents do if it is their child who is doing the bullying at school? And what should parents tell their child if he or she witnesses bullying going on? If you have reason to believe your child is bullying, the first thing for you to remember is *now = later*. If your child enjoys pushing weaker people around now and causing them injury, that is what he or she is likely to do as an adult, even with friends and partners. All social cruelty is formative this way, shaping the participant's behavior for the years ahead. Explain this to your son or daughter in preface to declaring why you are taking issue with their behavior now. "It is for the sake of your future relationships, so they don't come to harm, and you don't lose a friend or roommate or love interest that you value."

Now you have a fourfold agenda to follow, the same agenda you would follow if this middle school age son or daughter bullied a younger sibling at home:

1. Check out assumptions and excuses.

2. Reverse roles.

3. Evaluate the ethics.

4. Make amends.

First, you start by *checking out the assumptions and excuses* your child is making, comparing them to those that committed bullies typically hold to justify their hostile behavior. Hardcore bullies believe that they are superior, stronger, and entitled to rule, and they also believe that the victim is inferior, weaker, and deserving of mistreatment. This self-centered mentality seems to suggest, "All I care about is what happens to me; I don't care about what happens to you." Parents must ask a clarifying question: "Can you help me understand how you believe acting out toward this student was okay?" If the young person describes assumptions and makes excuses that support the bullying, then you need to specifically disagree by offering your own perspective to help the adolescent expand his or her own beliefs. You are not trying to win an argument. You want to create a discussion in which two different views of bullying can be shared.

Second, you should try *reversing roles*. You ask, "Suppose you were the other student being treated how you treated him, how might you feel?" The purpose of exploring this hypothetical role reversal is to help your early adolescent empathize with the victim and sensitize him or her to the emotional consequences of bullying. Bullies often have an overdeveloped focus on self-interest and an undeveloped sense of empathy for others. Consequently, there can be a limited capacity for sensitivity and remorse. Neither trait will serve the young person when he or she gets older and enters a significant relationship, be it romantic, marital, or parental.

Third, encourage an *ethical evaluation* of bullying. You want to help your early adolescent put the behavior in a moral context, because values endorse or censor how people choose to act. So you ask, "If everyone treated each other this way, would this be good or right to do?" And whether the answer is yes or no, open up a discussion: "Can you tell me more about why you believe that way?" Part of a parent's job is to help shape his or her child's and adolescent's sense of ethical responsibility.

Fourth, if after all this reflection, the young person considers bullying a wrong way to treat someone, then raise the possibility of *making amends*. Talk about what words might be said or actions taken to make retribution for what was done. The act of making amends can often make it more difficult to repeat the offense or injury again, because an effort was made to put wrongdoing right.

Finally, there remains what you should discuss with your middle school age child when he or she reports witnessing an incident of bullying at school. "These bigger guys stopped a smaller boy from passing in the hall, knowing they would make him late for class and get in trouble with the teacher. I was just walking by and could have interfered, but I didn't want to get involved. Besides, I didn't know what to do." What should parents say about the bystander's responsibility?

When it comes to observing any act of social cruelty, the old social activist statement about the citizen dilemma comes to mind: "If you're not part of the solution, you're part of the problem." Inaction around wrongdoing signifies complicity. Because interference feels risky, parents can sometimes help by honoring the risk but encouraging a response. "When you find yourself witness to bullying, you can always ask yourself this question: 'What is the least I could do or say that might make a difference?' For example, you might have done very little, but perhaps enough if you had simply stopped to let the bullies know someone was watching. Or you might have simply said something on the victim's behalf like: '*Oh, just let him go.*'"

Witnessing bullying poses one bystander problem, but reporting on the incident poses one that is even harder. Telling on a bully can divert the bully's attention to you. This threat of reprisal is how a bully can silence witnesses. When the assistant principal wants to know who started the fight, bystanders are often the "swing vote" in persuading these authority figures about what really happened. The bully claims innocence: "It wasn't me. All I did was say something kidding, and she (the victim) just freaked out and came after me. If you don't believe me, ask these students. They saw what she did." If your child is one of the witnesses and saw what really happened, will she lie like the other students to affirm the bully's story? If so, as often happens, the victim is likely to get punished and the bully set free. Acting to stop bullying directly as target and indirectly as witness both take social courage. From what I have seen, those young people who have outspoken, socially responsible parents tend to be the ones who, based on the modeling they have been given, are more likely to speak up and intervene when bullying occurs.

A victim of bullying described one such intervention: "I was stopped in the hall by three girls who wanted my lunch money when another girl, who's on the basketball team, just walked up, ignored them, took me by the hand, and said, 'Let's go,' and then she led me away. She didn't even look at the other girls, just at me. 'Let's go,' that's all she said. And maybe because she was so popular, seemed so confident, and acted like we were connected, they never bothered me again." As most bullying is done face-to-face, the next chapter describes the tactic of rumoring, where social cruelty is done indirectly and is often hard to trace.

CHAPTER SIX

RUMORING

Lara never discovered who started the rumor or why. Maybe someone envied her friendship with Celia and wanted to break them up. She first suspected something was wrong the night Celia wouldn't return her text messages, emails, or phone calls. So she called Kathleen, who hung up on her after saying Lara was two-faced and how no one would trust her again. Now what? So she called Lucia, who always knew all the gossip, and then Lara was told how she was seen talking with Flavio in the hall after class. "All we talked about was the class stuff, about when the next project was due."

"Sure," agreed Lucia, "but that's not what Celia knows. The word is out. You've got a crush on Flavio and are trying to break him and Celia up."

Lara felt helpless. The lie was spreading too fast to stop, and it got worse with each retelling, revealing something worse about Lara each time it was told. At school the next day, everyone had sided with Celia against her for being a backstabber and betraying a good friend, and no one wanted anything to do with her.

Rumoring is the creation and spreading of defamatory information that is usually partly or totally false to slander a person's reputation, reduce his or her social standing, and bring him or her down. Spreading rumors about someone makes the person telling it appear socially in the know, and it makes the object of the rumor look bad. Gossip is what spreads the hearsay of various rumors in the following ways:

- By *questioning* someone's behavior or motivation, rumor suggests something might not be right about the person. In so many words, the message could be "It makes you wonder if she's really hiding something."

- By *describing* someone in negative ways, rumor maligns a person's character. In so many words, the message could be "He's not the kind of person you can trust."

- By *accusing* someone of supposed wrongdoing, rumor blames the person for something he or she has not done. In so many words, the message could be "She was the one who caused the trouble."

- By *revealing* supposedly secret information about someone, rumor raises suspicion about the private side of a person. In so many words, the message could be "Do you know what I found out about him?"

- By *warning* about the supposed dangers of someone, rumor makes that person scary to be around. In so many words, the message could be "Don't get to close to her, because you might catch it."

- By *fabricating* a story about someone, rumor breaks a relationship or starts a feud or fight between people. In so many words, the message could be "I hear you've been talking trash about me, and I'm going to get you back!"

The power of rumor is that it can be:

- Negatively slanderous

- Difficult to trace

- Hard to verify

- Quickly spread

- Very difficult to stop

- Increasingly exaggerated with each retelling

- Given legitimacy with repetition

For adolescents, just like for adults, rumors are believed because they play on people's ignorance, fears, jealousies, longings, prejudices, grievances, resentments, and fantasies. At worst, rumor attempts character assassination. It becomes accepted as common knowledge about someone, damaging how that person is publicly known. Just like tabloid truths and urban legends (monster alligators in the New York City sewer system), rumor tends to be believed when unquestioned. Of course, our electoral process encourages the development and spreading of rumors to attack political enemies, so young people are schooled in rumoring by the adult society to some degree. Celebrities become actors in the stories that popular prejudice and imagination make up and convey about them, readily believed by people. Because it is so entertaining, the current rumor (spread by gossip) is treated as the latest, breaking news. When it comes to helping their son or daughter understand the psychology of rumoring, parents can pull from their own adult experience.

The Psychology of Rumoring

Rumor uses the magic of innuendo—creating the illusion of "fact" out of bits of history, unsubstantiated truth, and outright lies. Rumoring can be doubly destructive as well. First, rumor can injure young people's reputation by affecting how they are socially identified and valued, and second, rumor can injure their self-image, because how others see them may affect how they see themselves. If rumor about a boy, for example, spreads around the belief that "any team he's on is sure to lose," he may buy into rumor's content and start to believe that he is nothing but a liability. This is what happened to the gangly sixth grader who credited the rumors spread against him and decided not to go out for athletics.

Two kinds of rumors cause the most damage. There are *slanders* that attack reputation with lies, and there are *betrayals* that attack reputation by revealing what was supposed to be kept secret, violating privacy or breaking confidentiality. In either case, the object of the rumor feels slammed—exposed, attacked, and demeaned.

Being the object of rumor is scary. In the case of slander, adolescents often don't know who started the rumor and rarely find out who's spreading it. Neither do they know who believes it nor how to stop it. All they know is that people are talking about them in ways that hurt their reputation. Occasionally (I have only seen this in small private school settings, not in large public ones), it is possible to track down the source. Starting with the person from whom he or she first heard the rumor, the target will trace back its path by asking, "Who told you that about me?" And then, like following links in a chain, tracing one informant back to another, the adolescent will at last confront the story's initiator. "I know from other people you told that you started this rumor. I don't appreciate your spreading lies about me. I told the people you told that if you could do this to me, then you might do it to them. So stop starting rumors about me now!" In general, whether the school setting is small or large, when one has been "flamed" by a rumor, flaming someone back only keeps the rumors flying.

A rumor is like an advertisement: It is meant to *persuade*. It is intended to change or support existing beliefs about a person who is being slandered. Rumors are rarely complimentary; they are critical of the rumor's object. Because rumors seek the widest audience, they need to be repeated. They need to be retold to many people for the maximum effect. They are typically transmitted like a chain letter in the hopes that what is received will be passed on to others, most people unwilling to break the chain, some even eager to extend it. It is the sensational value of a rumor that makes them worth starting and worth spreading. People who easily believe rumors and automatically pass them along credit what they are told and do not stop, question, check, and think for themselves. The medium through which rumors are spread is gossip. However, gossip is not entirely bad. It serves a social function. It informally circulates information around a community—what is happening and who is doing what to whom—and it is broadcast every waking hour. To various degrees, people create it, listen to it, and pass it along as part of their normal interchange with each other. Gossip has the power to inform and entertain, and a person who is in possession of all the latest news can get a degree of social prominence, because he or she is really up on things. Students who are "rumor brokers" continually pass on everything they hear and can establish a valued social place. In the words of one young middle school informant: "I love gossiping about other people, but I hate it when they gossip about me." Most young people have mixed feelings about gossip.

But not all gossip is good. *Rumor is malicious gossip.* It is information intended to do somebody harm. At a meeting with middle school students, a young woman put it is this way: "Rumors come from students making up stories to hurt each other—that's what I think." And I agree. By shaping our understanding of others, rumors affect attitude and influence behavior, particularly attitude and behavior toward the person about whom the rumor is told. "When I heard what she had done, I didn't want any more to do with her!"

The Appeal of Rumors

Rumors are a hot topic in early adolescence. Being plugged into them is part of being in the social know. This is an age when young people invest an enormous amount of time in communication with each other to keep up with what is going on and what is being said, and this includes the latest rumors. It is also an age when feeling badly about yourself can make it easier to believe bad things said about others. At the very least, passing rumors along can distract young people from their own insecurities by focusing on the vulnerabilities of others. And they are often entertaining to those who are not being attacked.

Whether someone should believe a rumor or not all depends on how he or she feels about the teller and the rumor's object. In general, the more someone likes and trusts the teller, the more inclined he or she is to credit the rumor; and the more someone dislikes and distrusts the object of the rumor, the more inclined he or she is to want to believe it.

It's not the truth of rumors that is so persuasive, as that they are hard to prove false. Rumors are usually given the benefit of the doubt, because they *might* be true. Rumors gamble on possibility. Thus, many feuds and fights can be started when student A tells student B what student C has supposedly been saying about B, leading to a confrontation. B says, "I heard what you said about me!" Because the accusation is based on a false rumor, C doesn't know what B is talking about, but denial can sound defensive, so the fight often begins then, and A succeeds in disrupting that relationship.

Just as boys (primarily drawing esteem from competitive prowess) more frequently engage in physical bullying, girls (primarily drawing esteem from close relationships) more frequently engage in social rumoring. And because adolescent girls tend to enter puberty earlier than boys, the concern with acting and appearing womanly enough poses an early challenge to maintain a good enough reputation without attracting a bad rumor to tear that reputation down. Paraphrasing one young woman, she had to be "careful not to cross the line." And the line she described divided appearing adequately womanly from being provocatively sexual. Cross the line, and rumors could start about how she was "cheap," "trampy," "slutty," "trashy," or "sleazy." At this age, what people say about how she looks as a young woman can play havoc with her reputation.

There are a number of common motivations behind starting or spreading a rumor about someone:

- To bring down someone a person envies or dislikes
- To get back at someone who injured the person
- To break up someone's relationship
- To get someone in trouble
- To hurt the competition
- To attract attention

Wherever a lot of vicious rumors are passed around, some students will practice defensive socializing to stay out of harm's way. A young woman in eighth grade described her strategy for social survival this way: "I just try to be nice to people. I'm really careful about what I say. I don't get into crossways with anyone, and what's private, I keep to myself." That's the effect of rumors on a group. They put people on guard, and in the process, they increase suspicion and reduce openness and trust. Students start wondering if someone being nice is only acting fake and really conspiring against them. This state of distrust reminds me of that psychological saying, "Just because you're feeling paranoid doesn't mean that people are not really out to get you."

One of the problems of dealing with rumors is that they are often invisible to their target. As one student described it, "Rumors told behind your back can change how people treat you to your face." She should know, because it happened to her. All she noticed was friends treating her differently for no cause she could think of. They pulled away, stopped calling her or returning her calls, and when she approached a group of them, they would stop talking, as if they had been talking about her. As has been stated, rumors affect beliefs and beliefs affect behaviors, and their behavior toward her had definitely changed. In this case, she had the sense to suspect a rumor was at work, and getting with one of the friends alone, she didn't ask if there was a rumor about her going around; instead she acted like she knew there was. "What's the gossip about me now? I want to know!" And the friend reluctantly explained how the word was she had missed school getting treatment for a sexual disease from messing around and no one wanted to catch it. "Not true," explained the accused. "I had the flu. You can ask the doctor. And I don't mess around! So next time you hear something bad about me, please ask me instead of believing everything you're told."

Rumors told behind someone's back (as in, not to their face) is backstabbing. It is double-dealing and subversive when what friends say *to* other friends is different from what they say *about* other friends. It creates betrayal and suspicion. Can someone's friend really be an enemy? In one way, rumoring is the most destructive of the five kinds of social cruelty, because unlike the others, it is invisible—hard to source and trace. And yet rumor can ruin a person's reputation. In addition, it can also sew social distrust. For early adolescents who are already bedeviled with insecurity, rumoring makes this painful condition that much worse.

Reputation

Reputation is how a person is socially known and valued. It's what creates a first impression about people before anyone even gets to meet them.

What people first hear about someone can make an enormous difference: "I've heard she's really friendly" or "I've heard he's really sneaky." What early adolescents discover about reputation is disconcerting. Although it can strongly affect social standing, reputation is not in their control, even when that reputation is good. Reputation is what others choose to think about someone, and that is up to them, not up to the person who's reputation is being considered. As one student said, "Reputation is a daily thing. Some days you're up, and some days you're down. It depends on how you do and what people say about you."

Rumors attack reputation. Jealousy and envy are one major source of many rumors that are started. A very common target of rumoring is the *new student* who is particularly physically or socially attractive or who is a high athletic or academic performer. Whenever a new student enters a class of peers, he or she can unknowingly threaten to upset the established social pecking order. To keep the interloper from outshining the existing competition, rumors can begin sometimes before the target has even arrived.

"Do you know what I heard about him? At his last school, he got kicked out for using drugs. That's why he's here." The object of the rumors doesn't know why people are so stand-offish or unfriendly until the content of what has been said and spread gets back to him after a week or so. One well-dressed eighth grader described how "word got around that I had gone to a 'better school' and was really snobby, which isn't true! But nobody includes me or invites me to do anything." That's the ultimate damage rumor can do. Not only does it tarnish a person's reputation, but it affects the social treatment they are given. In this case, these new students didn't get to make a first impression, because rumor made it for them. Based on what other students were led to believe, getting to know him and her was not something that many wanted to do, at least not right away.

Fortunately, not everyone believes or cares about the rumors. As a result, parents need to tell their son or daughter entering a new school to remain patient and keep meeting people, because as friendships build, a social place will open and a good reputation will be more realistically established. "You don't have to live those rumors down," they can explain. "You just have to wait and wear them out by ignoring them and letting people get to know the person you really are."

Establishing the reputation you want during early adolescence can be particularly challenging, especially when one is trying to catch social hold. Young people discover how little influence they have over this very important part of their life. Thus, the rules of reputation can be a harsh lesson.

- The reputation people have has a lot to do with the treatment they are given.

- Nobody controls his or her own reputation; other people do.

- People can lead a spotless life and still have their reputation tarnished.

- Anybody can be slandered.

- People will believe what they want to believe about someone.

- People like believing the worst about each other.

- The truth about a person is what anybody decides that truth is.

A lot of other rumors are circulated to avenge being hurt. Early adolescence is a time when many childhood friends, even best friends, grow apart as they begin to differentiate themselves from how they used to be. Sometimes, turning hurt to anger, the rejected person will leak information that the rejecting person told in confidence to get back at him or her for leaving. When good friends break up, all previous commitments to keep past confidences are often off the table. The same dynamic is at work in "break ups" of girl-boy relationships, where the jilted person defames the person who did the jilting. "She broke up with me because I wouldn't lie to cover up what she was doing. You want to hear?"

Then there are rumors started just for the fun of it to cause trouble for someone. "We just thought it would be funny to see if we could get people to believe that about her," explained several friends. "It was just a joke. We never thought anyone would believe it or that she would get in trouble. So we started spreading a story that she was dealing drugs at school, and word got to the principal, who called her in and her parents too!" But the rumor got around so well that the assistant principal, who kept an ear to the ground, heard it and passed it up the ladder. It's not just adolescents that can be taken in by rumors; adults can be, too.

In general, the higher up you are on the popularity pyramid, the more rivals and envious others will generate rumors about you. (In the adult world, this is why tabloids attack celebrities, not social unknowns.) Ironically, it is the social unknowns who are most free from receiving this social cruelty, because nobody is interested in them. The quiet students who mostly keep to themselves during middle school tend to escape the ravages of rumor. Next among the unaffected are the students who simply have no ambition to be popular, who have defined self-interests and a few good friends, and who couldn't care less what other people have to say about them. The unknowns and the self-interested seem to be the most socially immune to rumors or the pain from rumors when they are told. The rumors that hurt the worst are those that attack major vulnerabilities.

Probably the most viciously hurtful rumors for early adolescents are those that discredit someone's young womanhood or young manhood and their developing sexual identity. When stories are spread that a young woman is insufficiently moral or sexually loose, the label used to attack her reputation is often "slut." When stories are spread that a young man is insufficiently masculine from appearing not strong enough or not acting tough enough, the label used to attack his reputation is often "gay." (It is generally not until high school that the term becomes truly homophobic.) Then there are people who embody the physical ideal. Envious rumors can attack girls who are particularly beautiful ("She had plastic surgery.") and boys that are strongly built ("He takes steroids."). The lesson is that popularity provides no protection from vicious rumors; in fact, popularity can bring them on.

The Internet

The simpler days of sending letters, passing notes, and posting insults on the bathroom walls at school that parents remember are gone. Now there is the meeting room, chatting, messaging, posting, blogging, twittering, and email possibilities the online world allows. The opportunities for sending threatening, demeaning, and denigrating verbal and visual communications have been wildly expanded. Times have changed since parents were growing through adolescence, and it's important for parents to understand how new computer and cell phone technology have altered and expanded how young people communicate with each other today.

The Internet is the greatest rumor mill ever invented. It hosts and carries all manner of fictions masked as truths. In a split second, the touch of a key can deliver slanderous information to a seemingly infinite list of online destinations. Rumor can spread like wildfire, as instant messaging becomes instant rumoring that scorches someone's reputation before they even know they've been burned.

What young people must understand is that there is no privacy, confidentiality, or secrets in cyberspace. There is no recall or deleting of what has been posted or sent. And any disclosure people make about themselves can be spread and used against them if others should so choose. The power of rumor on the Internet reminds me of the prophecy attributed to pop artist Andy Warhol: "In the future, everyone will be defamed." Today, with the arrival of the Internet, that "future" has arrived. Somewhere posted in cyberspace is something critical (and at least partly untrue) about almost everyone.

For the fun or meanness of it, peers can ensnare a person with rumors in countless ways, only limited by the imagination and inventiveness of young people at this very experimental age, with a machine that has endless possibilities at their fingertips. Consider just a few examples:

- They can organize a hostile email and messaging campaign against someone.

- They can create a false advertisement about someone's supposed sexual behavior or orientation.

- They can alter a photograph to misrepresent what someone is doing.

- They can create a "gotcha" website to demean and defame someone.

- They can copy and paste private messages and images to embarrass or compromise someone.

Early adolescence is an experimental age when creating new self-expression and social interaction is fun. And some of the "fun" young people have on the Internet is using social networking to exploit the seemingly infinite possibilities for slander, pretense, and other mischief.

Today, everyone, young and old, exists in two worlds—the real world and the virtual world. Many young people, used to gaming online, believe that in the virtual world one gets to play by a different set of rules. As one young man reported, "You can do things to people on the Internet that you can't do in real life." By this, he meant that he could say things to people and about people, could trick them, could pretend to be them, could break into their business, and could hide who he was. But what is done in the virtual world has real world consequences, and parents can use the discussion of online rumoring to help their early adolescent understand this.

How young people are depicted in the virtual world can have real world effects, because much of their reputation is now generated on the Internet, where so much gossip is exchanged and where rumors are so quickly created and spread. The parents' task is complex. They must advise their son or daughter not only about dealing with rumors circulated face-to-face, but also the more disembodied ones that flourish in cyberspace. At this insecure age, young people would rather rely on bad information about what is going on in their social world than tolerate ignorance from no good information at all. It is their anxiety that makes them so welcoming of rumors.

The Early Adolescent Rumor Mill

And it's not just rumors about each other, but rumors about school itself that affect children this age. Early adolescents are rumor prone, because creating worries are how they often manage their insecurities and fears. Combine the developmental changes that come from their separation from childhood with the challenges of more social independence in relationship to peers with the chemical and physical alterations of puberty, not to mention the transition from elementary to secondary instruction, and you'll see that young people have more than enough to worry about. Worries are just rumors one creates about what might happen for the worst. Worries are a good way to scare yourself, and despite bravado to the contrary, early adolescents have a lot of anxieties.

Specifically what kinds of rumors are middle school age students circulating in their heads? Consider common worries generated about the transition from elementary to secondary instruction, usually from fifth to sixth grades. Students leave behind the security of a single classroom teacher for multiple subject area teachers, none of who will ever get to know them as well as their elementary teachers did. Now their school life becomes more impersonal, more complicated, and more demanding, because there are more teachers to get along with and a greater variety and quantity of work to manage.

I've spoken with graduating fifth graders about what they fear as new sixth graders entering in a public middle school, and here are some common rumors they have worried themselves into believing:

- "Some students get lost, because the place is so big."

- "Some students are late to class, because the passing time between periods is too short."

- "Some students don't bring the right books to class and get in trouble with teachers who are mean and strict."

- "Some students can't get into their locker, because it's jammed or they can't remember their lock combination."

- "Some students don't fit in and don't make friends."

- "Some students don't wear the right clothes, and everybody notices."

- "Some students get bumped in the halls by bigger kids."

- "Some students get trapped in the bathrooms by older kids."

- "Some students never find anyone to hang out with before school or at lunch."

- "Some students can't keep on top of all the work and get held back."

- "Some students don't know all the rules and get in trouble."

- "Some students get picked on dressing for gym."

Worries are rumors that early adolescents use to predict problems for themselves. How does the early adolescent rumor mill work? It runs very simply and very effectively. Change (like becoming a secondary student) creates ignorance; ignorance creates fear of the unknown; fear of the unknown creates worries that anticipate the worst; and worries about the worst generate more fears. It's an unhappy merry-go-round, and parents need to help the entering sixth grader stay off the ride.

To allay rumors about entering a public middle school, parents can make sure their young person goes to orientation, locates friends attending the same school, and, if possible, joins a school club, organization, or sport so that there is an entry group to hang out with. The antidote to worries is confidence based on knowledge of what is true, what is not true, and what one can do. Therefore, parents can ask what their adolescents' worst worries are about entering middle school and dispel those that are *not* so. "You will be clearly told all the new rules you need to know, and in a couple days, you'll learn your way around." And they can help plan for possible worries, too. "Before school starts, you can practice with your combination lock so you know it by heart." One antidote to worry is confidence by finding ways to feel more in control.

Unfortunately, I believe it is the susceptibility to create worrisome rumors that also makes early adolescents easy believers of rumors generated by others. When someone is insecure or frightened, it is easy to believe the worst. Sensitive to the insecurities and fears of the age, there are some strategies parents can use to help the young person reduce the harmful power of rumors.

What Parents Can Do

Parents need to talk to their middle school age son or daughter about rumors—their nature, believing in them, and passing them onto others. They can begin by saying something like this: "Any time mean gossip is told to you that makes somebody not present look bad—and most rumors are not meant to do the rumored person any good—that usually means that there is an ugly rumor at work. Remember, you always have a choice when you are told a rumor. For example, you may choose to decline to hear it out, or you may express disbelief in the information, or you may refuse to pass it on." Parents can also educate their adolescents about the nature of rumors and advise them to evaluate the rumors they are told. They can consider giving guidelines such as the following:

- *Be realistic.* Since no one controls his or her own reputation, everyone can be slandered, and because they are envied, popular people attract the most rumors of all.

- *Be skeptical.* People shouldn't automatically believe everything negative about someone that they are told. They should ask themselves, "Does this story reasonably and logically make sense?"

- *Refuse to be manipulated.* When slanderous gossip comes to someone, he or she should ask, "Who would benefit from my believing this, and who would suffer from my believing this?"

- *Be independent.* People should decide for themselves.

- *Be warned.* Once one starts a rumor, he or she is powerless to stop it.

- *Refuse to listen.* One can simply say they're not interested in the rumor someone is spreading.

- *Don't participate.* When people pass along a rumor, they become just as guilty as the person who started it.

- *Don't retaliate.* When people rumor back for rumoring them, they will keep the rumors flying.

- *Understand gossips.* People should beware anyone who gossips to them, because he or she will also gossip about them.

- *Test what is told.* People can test any rumor they hear by asking yourself three questions: 1) How likely is it to be true? 2) Can it actually be checked out? and 3) Who is this rumor intended to harm?

A daughter is upset over what a friend said people are saying about her for always being the top achiever: "She cheats is how she does it!"

In tears, she tells her parents, "But I'm an honest person and would never do that. And now everyone thinks I have! They look at me and whisper. The next time I do well, they'll use my high grade against me! How am I supposed to live it down?"

In response, they tell their daughter, "Time helps. Rumors may not die, but they get old. And the older they get, the more they lose their sensational value. Newer ones about other people soon take their place. That's how gossip works. Fresh news beats old news. Just declare the rumor to be false, but don't argue against it, because that sounds as if you have something to defend. Then bide your time, because the rumor against you will pass."

Rumoring in the Internet is more complex to trace and harder to stop, so parents must be proactive with their son or daughter. They must include the topic in the general guidelines for managing their adolescent's life in cyberspace.

Parents should say up front, "Never spread rumors about anyone on the Internet, and if you ever become victim of rumors spread on the Internet, we want to know so that we can help you."

The anonymity that people feel on the Internet emboldens them to send and post what they would not say face-to-face. About online rumoring, parents can say this: "Just like if you are ever threatened on the Internet, if you ever become the object of ugly rumors on the Internet, please let us know. With your permission, we can make ourselves party to the communication so the cyber rumoring, like the cyber bullying, is brought to a stop. The people doing it may think it's fun being mean by threatening your safety or attacking your reputation, but it's not. Part of a parent's job is to support you and let the senders and posters of these rumors know that you are not alone. These aggressors need to be notified that we can trace them, that they are now dealing with us, and that they have given us data to proceed against them if they don't stop this activity right away."

Also give advice for minimizing one's exposure to harmful rumors on the Internet. One of the problems of Internet communication is that what is impulsively sent can have lasting consequences. What a young person says and sends in the joking, trusting, or emotional moment can be passed and posted for all to see. After breaking up with her best friend, a student is distraught at what followed: "She posted what I sent to her in private. She used it against me. Now everybody knows what I did, even though I only did it once. It's all over the Internet!" Rumor has accomplished its slanderous work.

Parents can sympathize with the hard lesson. Their advice could be the following: "Don't send anything over the Internet you don't want the world to know or that you will later have a hard time living down. There is no guaranteed confidentiality or privacy on the Internet. And the half-life of whatever words or images you send is virtually forever. Therefore, never send anything over the Internet that can possibly be used against you."

If your child was involved in the rumoring by passing it along, you can talk to him or her about taking a share of the responsibility and acting to right the situation. This can include apologizing to the target who was hurt, recanting the rumor, and trying to get others to stop spreading information that is destructively untrue. Adolescents can learn some powerful lessons when this is done:

- It's harder to stop a rumor than it is to start one.

- Apologizing does not relieve the injury that has been done.

- Telling those who told the rumor that it's a lie only injures one's reputation.

- Asking others still spreading the rumor to stop makes one unpopular with them.

Having gone through this process of restitution, the young person is less likely to welcome rumors others tell or collaborate in spreading them again.

One of the hallmarks of early adolescence is the propensity to criticize and the reluctance to compliment parents, siblings, or peers. At this time of insecurity, self-consciousness, and fragile self-esteem, it is hard to say something sincerely complimentary to another person when feeling so unsure of oneself. This tendency to criticize is part of what makes young people so welcoming of rumors. By spreading them around and bringing other people down, they can feel like they are bringing themselves up as a result.

Young people who are securely self-connected, however, are not only less bothered by rumors about them and less prone to pass along rumors about others, but they also have enough esteem to compliment others. And when they give compliments, they make a positive contribution to the social climate at a time when many of their peers are negatively disposed. Therefore, you should encourage your son or daughter to be a giver of compliments, not a spreader of criticism. It will do everyone some good.

Mean words spoken to someone can hurt, but lying words told about him or her to someone else can hurt the worst of all, particularly when those words are believed and spread through gossip as if they were the truth. When a number of people conspire to spread lies about someone, that is one way ganging up is done. Ganging up both amplifies the effect of the other four social cruelty tactics—teasing, excluding, bullying, and rumoring—and it is a tactic unto itself. It can feel very threatening and very lonely to know that a group dislikes a person and may act against him or her when it suits their collective will. The next chapter describes the obvious (and not-so-obvious) harm that the social cruelty tactic of ganging up can cause.

CHAPTER SEVEN

GANGING UP

Mad at Keisha for not inviting her along with everybody else, Lucy started telling friends how hurt she was to be left out. "How would you feel?" she asked. The more friends listened and sympathized with Lucy, the more they allied themselves with her position. They believed Lucy was right to feel wronged, and the more they supported her, the more hostile they felt toward Keisha, who started feeling ganged up on for what she had done. Lucy managed to turn a social loss into a social gain. She had more friends on her side than before. Now it was Keisha's turn to feel outnumbered.

On its most basic level, ganging up is in fact a numbers game. The more friends people have to back them, the more socially powerful they are. To truly have a "gang of friends" creates security at an insecure age. However, it is also a fractious and fickle age. Fallings-out between friends and the realignment of friendships are an everyday part of this changeable period of life. Disagreements between young people can shift patterns of social allegiance, as people choose to pick one person's side over the other's. In this way, *ganging up* lobbies for social loyalty to organize social support.

This is the age when hate clubs can be formed. "Let's all hate Jamie," someone dominant suggests, and now others agree to join the hate club. "We'll call ourselves the *We Hate Jamie Club*." Often the person in Jamie's place has done nothing to incite the hostility. She just serves as a convenient target for getting free-floating aggression out. As for Jamie, it's very lonely to be hated collectively.

On its most harmful level, those ganging up can decide to aggress against an individual using any (or any combination of) the other four kinds of social cruelty—teasing, exclusion, bullying, rumoring—to demean, ostracize, injure, or defame the person. Now, because the social cruelty is no longer one-on-one but many-against-one, the effects are greatly amplified. To the victim, it can become overwhelming. It's one thing to have a bully wait to taunt or shove a student when he or she boards the school bus, but it's quite another to run a gauntlet of pushes and shoves and trips by the bully or all her buddies as the student stumbles down the aisle to reach a seat at the very back. Ganging up makes teasing more scornful, exclusion more isolating, bullying more threatening, and rumoring more slanderous.

Ganging up to deliver social cruelty is a very serious numbers game calculated to accomplish the following:

- Communicate mass dislike: "Everybody hates you!"

- Create a common object of ridicule: "They all laugh at me!"

- Conspire to blame: "We'll swear she started it."

- Organize greater power: "He can't stand up to us."

- Build group solidarity: "Let's all go after her!"

Ganging up can often come as a surprise, at least to the victim. It did for Jay, who was feeling really good about himself for getting to hang out with the older guys, even invited to join in their adventures. But when the principal discovered what "somebody" did (sprayed graffiti on the girl's room stall in this case), suddenly they all agreed he was the one to blame. Now it was their word against his.

Those ganging up feel more powerful from being part of a concerted social action. The person ganged up on feels more helpless from having so many people unite against him or her. At worst, when the group attacks an individual for being different (from the group) in race, ethnicity, religious faith, language, sex, sexual orientation, disability, or like character-istics, then cruelty can be socially intensified. The poison of prejudicial stereotypes ("He's one of them!") and the power of discrimination ("His kind deserves beating up!") can result in injury from harassment ("Let's get him!"). Verbal and physical attacks by jocks on boys who appear insufficiently masculine and are labeled effeminate or gay still occur, although this is less common in middle school than high school. To defend their maleness, the attackers punish and degrade the attacked.

The Psychology of Ganging Up

Ganging up demonstrates how young people who are individually capable of good can collectively commit harm. And because the action is collective (a group of large boys pummeling a smaller one on the playground, for example), they can disown full responsibility for what happened by blaming it on "just going along with what everyone else was doing."

The most common motivations for ganging up seem to be *punishing* or *persecuting*. Ganging up to give punishment is usually done because the victim has violated a condition of group membership or betrayed the group trust. For example, by reporting another student in the group for cheating on a test, the informant is given a name it takes her a long time to live down. In fact, whenever they are angry with her, they still bring it up. "Rat," they call her. Ganging up to persecute is usually because the victim displays characteristics others are fearful of possessing themselves. For instance, a group of boys may tease another who has a speech impediment and is not verbally fluent enough to meet their standards of verbal banter. They punish the offending trait by all making fun of the stuttering offender ("Hey Stut, speak to us!") to show it's him, not them. Physical handicaps, learning disabilities, and emotional vulnerabilities can attract ganging up, because by tormenting the offender, the tormenters affirm how they are different from, and superior to, the victim.

Ganging up can bring out the worst in young people, because they will commit acts of social cruelty together that they would never do individually. That "everybody else is doing it" encourages, endorses, or at least excuses participating in mistreatment to some degree. Shared responsibility reduces the individual sense of blame. Members feel freer to do what they individually would not. As one young woman defended her actions, "I only trashed her locker because that's what the other girls were doing. It's not my fault. I didn't start it. I just went along." Ganging up creates a group mentality that is hard for individual members of the group to resist.

"Why did you go along?" I asked.

Her answer was painfully true. "I was scared to go along, but I was more scared not to." *These frightened followers are the secondary victims of ganging up.*

When students say that they were only joining in the punishment or persecution, that reminds me of a definition a young person once gave me: "Ganging up is piling on." So when one girl gets mad at another, she may lobby friends over to her side to oppose or punish the other girl. Ganging up often begins by getting others to choose one's side. Then group teasing, exclusion, bullying, or rumoring can begin. The shifting alliances around fights, jealousies, grievances, break ups, and boyfriends can create a lot of drama during the middle school years for girls among whom social ganging up can often occur.

"Who needs all this unnecessary drama?" a mother asked. She was tired of her daughter's worry with all the social goings-on that preoccupied and upset the girl much of the time. And she was impatient with all the phoning, texting, and messaging that took up the girl's evening time. But these conversations about who is saying what about whom, who is breaking up and making up, who is getting hurt and getting payback, as well as who is getting mad and staying mad are not needless or pointless. They are part of the serious jockeying for relationships and place in what can be a chaotic social world, where little things matter a lot because they can become big so fast. "Just because I didn't greet you back in the hall you told everyone I was acting like a snob!"

So I asked the mother who was "tired of this nonsense," "Where you work are there office politics that you need to keep up with?"

"Sure," she replied. "If I didn't stay plugged in, I'd get blindsided or edged out."

"Well," I explained, "your daughter's world isn't a whole lot more different from that, except it's more complex. She has less life experience, and she is more vulnerable to getting hurt." Parents need to treat these dramatic ups and downs with respect and sensitivity.

From what I have seen, ganging up is a common act of

social cruelty. It is not as gender-specific as bullying often is for boys and exclusion often is for girls. The major sex-related difference in ganging up is how it is often done—boys tending to use physical means, girls tending to use social ones.

For example, there is the group of seventh grade boys that have a game they play called "Popping Willy." Willy is a big kid, but he's very mild-mannered and shy, and he doesn't have many friends at school. Each day, one of this gang of boys takes his turn to "pop Willy," which means squaring off and punching him really hard while the other guys watch. Willy never knows when it is going to happen, but he always knows that sometime during the day it will in fact happen. And when it does, there will be a group of guys standing around to clap and laugh. Physical ganging up is something these boys enjoy.

At the eighth-grade boys' basketball game, there is a group of five slender girls seated on the top of the riser, each with her cell phone, talking and texting and laughing. They are all dressed in the same kind of fashionable tight tops and jeans. On the lowest riser sits another girl alone, heavyset and wearing loose-fitting clothes, and not done up like the other five. She is holding her cell phone that is continually buzzing as a barrage of text messages keep coming her way. She is not laughing. She is not looking around. From my on-looking perspective, it appears she is receiving a steady flow of cruelty from the other five, probably all making fun of how she looks and how she's dressed. Finally, she gets up and walks out of the gym, driven off. Social ganging up is something these girls enjoy. Having succeeded to this degree, think of how much "fun" they could have making the offending girl's life worse by organizing a smear campaign against her on the Internet.

Students hang with the gang and act with the gang, because the gang makes them bigger. Being a member of a group has many advantages:

- There's size in numbers.

- There's safety in numbers.

- There's support in numbers.

- There's strength in numbers.

- There's sanctuary in numbers.

- There is always something to do in numbers. (One never has to worry about getting bored.)

In almost every act of ganging up, everyone suffers. The obvious party that suffers is the victim; but no less affected can be members of the group who participate, not because they really want to but because they feel they have to go along with the group. That's the power of the group in early adolescence, when belonging becomes so important. At issue is how to manage all the vulnerabilities that come with feeling different— from how one was as a child, from the changes of puberty, from one's peers. The power of group membership is that it allows

"I" to become "we." Young people can also congregate and affiliate themselves with a group of peers who are all, in some significant ways, "different" the same way they are, making differentness acceptable. "We are all alike." The early adolescents' social goals are to find a group of their own kind, stick to their own kind, stand up for their own kind, and go along with their own kind, and that can include ganging up.

Young people go along for two reasons: *social conformity* and *social obedience*. There is a rich psychological literature explaining how the power of these social dynamics can influence human behavior. For insecure early adolescents concerned about establishing their social place, consider how these forces can play out.

There is the need for social conformity with peers in order to fit into the group. This need is accompanied by the *fear of rejection* for not doing so. In the quest for fitting in, authenticity is often sacrificed, proven by the complaint "I can't just be myself."

There is the need for social obedience to ruling peers in the group in order to maintain good standing with the powers that be. In succumbing to social obedience, freedom of choice is often sacrificed, demonstrated by the complaint "I have to follow the crowd." This need is accompanied by the *fear of reprisal* for not doing so. Appearing too individual or acting too independent can be costly.

The goth student who comes to school in his white oxford shirt just for the sake of variety, or the new student who challenges the queen bee of her group to speak her mind, can both be in for a hard day with their respective peers. The first has committed a breach of uniform; the second had committed a breach of deference. During early adolescence, the need to establish a social place among one's peers is very strong. A teacher's observation about this comes to mind. "Going to school at this age can feel like going to prison, at least in terms of the potential for danger from the hostility you face. You are an inmate of people from whom you cannot get away. You have to keep company with them each day. So for your own protection, you better find a group to belong to."

When your group of friends is ganging up on someone, it can be very hard not to go along with them, much less to speak out against what is going on. If parents get word that their son or daughter has elected to avoid participating or even stepped in to side with someone being ganged up on by the group, they must appreciate the courage that this takes and say so. The phrase "lonely are the brave" really applies. Ganging up is a numbers game, where the person outnumbered gets hurt.

Victims of Ganging Up

By definition, victims of ganging up do not have numbers on their side. If not isolated, they only have a few friends, and these are not likely to be socially popular or powerful enough to stand up for them. There's a kind of chicken and egg phenomenon that entraps the victim in many ganging up situations. Is the adolescent a victim because he or she has few friends, or does the young person have few friends because he or she is a victim (and other students don't want to catch that vulnerability from the target)? The answer is usually some of both.

In the middle school grades, there will always be students cast as the victim of ganging up, because the social role is so badly needed for young people beset by insecurity. To those ganging up, this student often personifies traits that nobody else wants attributed to them—weird, stupid, slow, fat, weak, unmanly, unwomanly, oversensitive, all the kinds of traits that people feel insecure about. By aggressing against the victim, those ganging up make it look like they are different from the person they are attacking. Thus, *the victim both becomes the repository and protector of their fears*, keeping others safe from this mistreatment by taking it on him or herself. The boy who cries easily, the girl who is self-consciously overweight—both embody major fears that same-sex peers harbor at this age.

To complete the twisted thinking that justifies ganging up, there are several common ways to blame the victim:

- "She deserved it."
- "He was asking for it."
- "She let it happen."

These statements shift responsibility to the object of the ganging up.

In some instances, school authorities act as if it's easier to blame the victim for bringing the cruelty on than sanctioning the whole group of students who were doing the ganging up (and then dealing with all their parents). That's one problem with ganging up; the numbers rule because they have so many people on their side. The school authorities may be more inclined to take the words of many against the word of one. As a student who had been ganged up on in this way bluntly put it, "The teacher believes the liars, because there are more of them! I didn't do it, but there's just one of me!"

Sometimes teachers can encourage students to gang up on another person by how they maintain discipline in the classroom. One strategy is to penalize every student for the infraction of one. The coach says, "Anybody drops the ball, and everyone does wind sprints." Or the teacher says, "Just one person talks, and everyone is kept after." If one student can't seem to stop dropping the ball or talking, a lot of peer resentment is developed and possibly directed against him or her. The worst setup I ever heard about was a fifth grader who the teacher liked so well she gave the girl a special job. She announced to the class, "I have to leave the classroom for fifteen or twenty minutes, and I want you all to do your work while I'm gone. I've asked Amanda to write on the board the names of anyone who misbehaves." The teacher chose

Amanda because she was so obedient; and because she was so obedient, Amanda did as the teacher asked, having written seven names on the board by the time the teacher returned, and those seven students were kept after school. The next day, Amanda was beaten up. Accepting the teacher's assignment of responsibility, she had earned their enmity.

Street gangs carry social conformity and social obedience to an extreme degree. These dynamics are what make initiation so formative, membership so strong, exiting so difficult, and experiences of ganging up more likely to occur—expressing loyalty to and solidarity with the group. In some middle schools, students may already start to become members of gangs. Gangs attract members among early adolescents, because young people are at a prime recruiting age. For young adolescents, the association with and protection of older students is highly valued. Nine- to thirteen-year-old people join them for social security, identity, status, protection, and independence. More tightly knit than a group or a clique, a gang is an abandoned youth group for whom peers become the primary social affiliation when salient adults have become harder to relate to, distant, or absent. Now extreme social independence rules. Despite the prejudicial stereotype in response to the racial homogeneity of many gangs (there are gangs of every race), race does *not* create gangs. *Adolescence causes gangs* in the same way it causes cliques and groups. In addition, there are not just inner city gangs, but also suburban gangs, wannabes who thrill to imitate the outlaw ways of their urban counterparts.

The point here is not that all early adolescents, particularly boys, join street gangs. They don't. But most early adolescents of both sexes strive to become part of a peer group that has the potential for ganging up. And when this happens, members engage in a unifying, collective act of hostility where "group-think" takes over and individual judgment and responsibility are surrendered. In the moment, social momentum causes everyone to feel more like a follower than a leader.

Ganging up is a socially formative experience, because every time your child participates in ganging up, he or she becomes more closely tied to the group and to the values and conduct for which it stands. Ganging up increases similarity. The mental set of the individual begins to match that of the group. Asked how she could participate in such a collective act of cruelty, a remorseful seventh grader just shook her head in bewilderment: "I must have lost my mind!" In the heat of the moment, she did. There are cases where the young person keeps his or her presence of mind but goes along to belong. Because his new friends like to scare a student who becomes easily frightened, a seventh grader joins in the "fun" of group intimidation to be accepted as part of the crowd, even though he doesn't think it is right.

Perhaps this loss of individual and family mind-set may partly explain an incident widely reported in the news media.

While a group of middle school age girls took turns beating up another girl, one of them filmed the mistreatment and then posted it on the Internet to publicize and celebrate what they had done. The April 12, 2008, *New York Times* headline read: "Teenagers Charged with Beating Have Their Day on the Web." At that time, the girls were each released on a bail of $30,000 each. Even though this conduct is inconsistent with how they were taught to treat people at home and how they individually believed, ganging up encouraged these actions to occur because the peer frame of reference prevailed.

This is the risk in early adolescence. In search of social independence, young people will shift more identification, attachment, and influence to peers. That shift is necessary for some separation from childhood and family to occur. What is not necessary, however, is for parents to surrender to the separation and hand over primary social control to this new cohort of age-mates. Parents and family must remain the primary source of reference and model for conduct in the young person's more independent social world. They must not bow out, because when they do, pressure and social values and direction from the group, clique, or gang takes over. Then the young person is allowed to become too independent for his or her own good, switching families run by parents to the one run by friends. The more distant from parental influence, the more easily swayed by peers he or she becomes. Abandonment by adults at this fragile and socially susceptible age is dangerous for the early adolescent who mistakenly believes that this is just the freedom he or she wants and needs.

So the question is, how can parents maintain a sufficient sense of place when their child is so powerfully drawn into the company of peers? I believe the young people most likely to get involved in ganging up are the children of parents who have lost their salience in the life of their son or daughter. *If your early adolescent participates in an act or acts of ganging up, that should be a wake-up call for you to bring the young person back into the family fold.* When your child participates in ganging up, as follower or leader, the power of peers is too great and the influence of parents is too slack.

What Parents Can Do

The first thing to understand is that parents are not powerless compared to the influence of peers. What parents need to do is strengthen the young person's capacity to retain individual and family frame of reference during a time when fitting in and going along with peers becomes much more tempting. So how can parents strengthen their own influence and the young person's judgment? For starters, try consistently insisting on and supporting the "eight anchors for family influence." These anchors are completing homework, cleaning up one's room, doing household chores, joining family activities, contributing community service, saving money, developing proficiency, and relating to salient adults.

From what I have seen in counseling over the years, parents who subscribe to the importance of these behaviors tend to raise an adolescent who maintains a sense of family place and frame of reference upon which to call when out making decisions among their friends. Individually, each anchor is helpful, and taken together, they provide significant stabilizing power. Notice that each one is accomplished independently of the group thinking of peers and so provides the young person another influence on his or her thoughts, values, and conduct. After listing each one, I suggest the influential contribution that is made.

- *Completing homework.* Separate from any academic value, fulfilling this nightly study obligation provides *work ethic training.* By exerting sufficient strength of will to do what is in one's best interest when it is not what one wants to do can develop self-discipline.

- *Cleaning up one's room.* At a more messy age, this instills the principle of *living on parental terms.* By abiding by their desire (and supervision) for order in the home, a young person consents to go along with what matters to them.

- *Doing household chores.* Unpaid, this regular investment of energy and effort meets *family membership requirements.* By investing in home maintenance and support, the young person becomes a valued contributor to the family.

- *Joining in family activities and gatherings.* Socially participating in family events affirms *primary social affiliation.* By joining in these activities, the young person is reminded of the abiding importance of family over the pressing (and often passing) value of peers.

- *Volunteering for community service.* Participating within a larger social good shows *concern for the welfare of others.* Demonstrating responsibility one has for those in need within the larger community, the young person becomes less self-centered and appreciates having help that is worth offering.

- *Saving money.* Putting away some earned money instead of immediately spending it is a lesson in *delaying gratification.* Exercising self-restraint, even planning ahead, the young person learns to resist the impulses and temptations of the moment.

- *Developing proficiency.* Cultivating interests and capacities through application and practice *builds competence.* Working to do something well or know something thoroughly, the young person builds self-esteem and self-confidence.

- *Relating to salient adults.* Enjoying the company of significant adults who are not one's parents creates the opportunity for *grown-up, influential friends.* In these older relationships, the young person is offered a more mature frame of reference to respond to and live up to than that offered by his or her peers.

Do I know for sure if these eight "anchors" will steady adolescent growth against the pressures of peer group membership? No. But what I do know is this: A young person is much more likely to fall under the sway of peers if he or she never does the following:

- Never does homework

- Never cleans up his or her room

- Never does household chores

- Never participates in family activities

- Never contributes community service

- Never saves money

- Never develops any proficiency

- Never befriends salient adults

As for which is worse, being victims or followers when ganging up occurs, both are bad. For the victims, there is often the sense that the world has turned against them. For the followers, there is often the sense of being swept up by the collective motivation of the group. In both cases, a sense of powerlessness in the situation can result. What can parents do should their son or daughter become a victim of ganging up or participate in ganging up? Start with your child as victim first.

The first priority for parents should be to *act empathetic*— listen and hear out the young person's emotions. This mistreatment is scary, lonely, and hurtful, and the young person needs support from a loving family. Then, parents need to *focus on what meaning* their son or daughter is attaching to what happened. For example, an adolescent's self-worth may have taken a tumble from the ganging up, and now the young person makes statements such as the following:

- "Nobody likes me!"

- "What a loser I am!"

- "I'll never have any friends!"

- "What's the matter with me anyway?"

Parents need to weigh in. "When you've been mistreated is no time to treat yourself badly. That's like believing that there must be something wrong with you when other people treat you wrongly. And that's not so. It's the guys who were ganging up on you that have something wrong with them. Thinking well of yourself when you've been hurt this way can be difficult, but that is what we want you to do. Otherwise you join the ganging up against yourself."

Or suppose the young person is angrily indulging revenge fantasies:

- "If it's the last thing I do, I'll get them back!"

- "I'll make them sorry for what they've done!"

- "I'll hate them forever!"

- "They better watch out!"

Parents need to weigh in on these responses as well. "We are angry about what happened, too. But getting back at them makes you no better than them. We'd rather work with you to find a way to stop this ganging up from happening again."

Many times the victim of ganging up will generalize in ways that make a hard experience worse. "Everyone has turned against me. No one likes me. I have no friends. All anybody wants to do with me is hurt me." If that list of suppositions were true, then the young person would be in a hopeless situation, so parents need to gently challenge the overgeneralization that fear and pain have made.

In reality, how many students were in the group ganging up? Usually it is an identifiable few. Not "everyone" joined in. Other friendships and acquaintanceships are unaltered, and this is a time to affirm and build on those relationships with other peers at school.

When ganging happens to their child, parents must help the young person activate other companionships and friendships where their son or daughter experiences what it is like to be an accepted, respected, and valued member of a group. This is why a young person needs multiple outside social circles to belong to, particularly during early adolescence when relationships can get so cruel at school.

Parents also need to ask, "Were these friends who turned against you or not friends who decided to get you? If they were people considered friends, are there other friends who did not participate? Maybe it is worthwhile to spend more time with friends who were not involved. Concerning the friends who were ganging up, was it a response to something you may have done?"

"Yes, I told on someone when I shouldn't have."

Ganging up by students who are not friends can be a different story, particularly if the mistreatment happens on a continual basis. Your son or daughter has been cast in the role of easy victim who will absorb their hostility. In this case, school becomes a really punishing and scary place. Your son may have tried to stop the ganging up by approaching a couple of the members of the bullying group individually. In doing so, he declared his wish not to be treated this way; he explained how it hurt, and he asked the person to persuade the others to please stop.

If the ganging up continues, however, parents need to approach the school authorities in an advocating, not attacking way. That is, they are there to represent the safe interests of their son; they are not there to accuse the school or blame the perpetrators. They should be calm, objective, reasoned, reasonable, determined, and insistent.

And they should be extremely well-informed. They should document what has specifically happened, when exactly these incidents occurred, who witnessed the events, and who were the individuals involved. Then they are willing to work with the school staff, but if that proves insufficient they must also be willing to go through channels to higher levels of authority in the system. No school likes trouble with parents, so if parents are willing to make persistent, *reasonable* trouble on their child's behalf, they are usually able to get the corrective attention they need.

Sometimes, telling parents about repeated ganging up at school can result in the parents simply letting the school know what is happening, and the authority at school can put a stop to it. An eleven-year-old boy never got to eat his lunch for two weeks, because a group of three boys always sat next to him and pretended to play takeaway with his food, daring him to stop them, which of course he didn't. For the three, it was their lunchtime entertainment. For the one, it was his lunchtime dread. Finally, when he told his parents and the parents told the principal and the principal told the lunchroom monitor, this lunchroom "play" came to an end. Young people need to know that they can call on parents to be advocates on their behalf, particularly when repeated ganging up situations occur.

However, in the event that parents are unable to get ganging up to stop, or in the event that their son or daughter is too emotionally damaged by the situation to recover a sense of safety with peers, parents may opt for a "geographic cure." They may want to transfer their child to a different school within the district or to another district entirely. Sometimes this change works for the good, because the young person is able to establish a new reputation and relationships free from the torment and tormenters in the old school situation. Young people may need parental help when recovering from victimization by ganging up; they may also need help from parents to assess the costs of joining in.

What can parents do when their early adolescent joined in the ganging up? The first major question to ask your son or daughter is "Would you have behaved this way if you had been acting alone?" If the answer is "no" (and it usually is), then you need to have a discussion about violating personal values and following the forces of the group. Did the young person feel a need to *fit in* (social conformity) to be like everybody, or else? Did he or she feel a need to *go along* (social obedience), to do like everybody, or else? And how did adolescents feel about their actions when the episode of ganging up was over? Did they feel good about themselves? Or did they experience any regret or remorse? Given the same set of circumstances, would they act that way again? The transforming effect that group behavior can have on individual choice is at issue here. Ganging up hurts the victim with the collective force of group hostility, but it also hurts group members by causing them to sacrifice individual responsibility and act together how they each might not normally act alone.

Having addressed the issue of individual responsibility for joining in, parents then need to address the issue of empathy for the victim. Those young people who are comfortable letting the will of the group decide for them and who don't care about the effects of their collective cruelty on the victim are most likely to participate in ganging up again.

The second major question to ask your son or daughter is "How would you feel if you were in the victim's place?" You want to emotionally sensitize the young person to the personal consequences of what was done. Then move into ethical evaluation. "In your heart of hearts, do you believe treating someone this way is right? If so, can you tell me why? If not, can you tell me why?" And finally, based on his or her own empathy and ethical evaluation, see if your son or daughter is willing to restore some justice to what happened by making amends with the victim. "What could you do for the victim to partially make up for harm that you have done?" An early adolescent who repeatedly follows the group in ganging up is more likely to become an adult who is socially conforming and socially obedient at his or her expense. You want your early adolescent to understand that a majority decision by his or her group of peers doesn't make a wrong decision right.

Whether it's ganging up, teasing, exclusion, rumoring, or bullying, most of these acts of social cruelty among early adolescents occur at school. This is the institutional gathering place where five days a week, nine months a year, they spend more time with peers than they often do sharing active company with parents at home. It is not enough for parents to counteract social cruelty from the family; the school must be actively involved in supporting prevention there as well. The next and final chapter discusses some ways school staff can act to reduce the incidents of social cruelty in the lives of middle school age students.

CHAPTER EIGHT

WHAT THE SCHOOL CAN DO

Many years ago, another consultant and I were called in to help a small rural school district (one with a single kindergarten through high school campus) and its staff deal with a certain problem they never had before. According to the principal, "All the students are saying really mean things to each other. These are good kids. I know them all, and I know they are not happy about what is going on. What I don't know is why they're treating each other this way or how to stop it." Then she described a growing problem of students saying hurtful things to each other, a practice that seemed to have started at the beginning of the year among sixth graders. Now it was infecting all the upper grades, and it was starting to influence how students treated each other in the grades below. "Whatever it is," said the principal, "it appears to be catching." As she gave us incidents for examples, the social cruelty seemed to be confined to one tactic alone—teasing. A culture of put down and cut down had somehow been created, and now students attacked each other with insults in their own defense to preempt being attacked first. Armed with this information, we spent a day with the sixth through twelfth graders in the gymnasium to help them examine how they were treating each other, how it felt, and how they might treat each other differently to feel better. Essentially, we started the process (that teachers continued) of re-norming the students' relationships with each other by identifying the hurtful behaviors they wanted to stop, and by choosing, and practicing more friendly behaviors they wanted to start.

Although parents have an important role to play at home helping their early adolescent avoid committing acts of social cruelty and providing support should such acts come his or her way, it is important that school staff confronts this problem because they have these young people in their care for so much of the day. This final chapter suggests some actions that school staff might want to take to combat this problem.

It takes a strong teacher to work with young people during the middle school years, when every student is breaking out of childhood and entering into adolescence. Middle school students are difficult to teach, because there is so much change going on in their early adolescent lives, including the following:

- The transition from elementary to secondary education, where more responsibility is expected for keeping up with more schoolwork from more teachers, and keeping company with a larger collective of students.

- The separation and differentiation from childhood, during which one has to give up some old dependencies and definitions and begin to establish a new independence and identity.

- The challenge of acting older, during which more worldly understandings and experiences must be dared and mastered.

- The physical and chemical transformations of puberty, during which one's appearance dramatically alters in ways one can't control.

- The increased intolerance of parental limits and demands, during which time more conflicts over freedom develop at home.

- The complexities of a more independent social world, where one's membership in a separate society of peers becomes more important and difficult to establish.

Insecure, self-conscious, and vulnerable on account of all these changes, young people are also more aggressive with each other to protect themselves and establish their social places. Just as they are more actively and passively aggressive with parents at home, using argument and delay to resist parental authority, they are also more socially aggressive with each other at school.

Early adolescents push more with each other. Now there is pushing to provoke, pushing for control, pushing against competition, pushing to get ahead, pushing to flirt, pushing back against being pushed, and pushing around to establish dominance. In an independent world of peers, they have to become more socially aggressive to make their way. *When aggression with each other is calculated to hurt each other, social cruelty results.* A young person's greatest exposure to acts of social cruelty occurs at that largest and most regular gathering place for early adolescents and their peers, namely the school.

Years ago, a middle school teacher at a workshop cracked a joke that was halfway serious: "I think we ought to declare a moratorium on teaching kids this age and then wait a few years until the changes settle down and they get their concentration back." He was describing how hard it was to command their attention with so many natural distractions from growth and social change going on. Then another teacher cut to some of the social cruelty issues: "And while we're at it, what about a rumor control center for girls and a fight referee for boys?"

It's true. At this vulnerable age, treating other people badly to manage feeling badly about themselves, young people can mistreat each other more seriously than they did before. At the same time, there is a window for instructional influence at this stage of development, as students struggle to figure out how to construct and conduct a more independent social world and also determine how to treat each other within it. There is an educational opportunity for the school staff working with middle school children to directly impact the social development of early adolescents.

To ask school staff to incorporate yet another educational effort into an already overcrowded agenda of curricular responsibilities is an imposition when they already have more than enough to accomplish. However, doing nothing about social cruelty only contributes to a lack of student safety. This sense of jeopardy can interfere with learning and shape student behavior with each other for worse mistreatment later. Schools that turn a blind eye to social cruelty pay an academic price through lost student attention to instruction, and they lay the groundwork for more serious social problems for these young people later in life.

Why would staff turn a blind eye? Because some adults are truly blind. Feeling that school is a safe experience for them, they assume that it feels safe to students. Such an illusion denies the reality of social competition, rivalries, collisions, provocations, taunts, insults, rumors, offenses, grievances, grudges, threats, injuries, worries, and fears that can become part of young people's daily school life during the middle school years. The world of staff is not the same as the world of students. *Staff and students live worlds apart in the same school.*

In schools, as in social groups of any kind, there is always pressure on individual members to conform to the dominant social norm. The significant question to ask is "Who gets to set this norm?" At school, if staff let students set their early adolescent norms of peer interaction, social cruelty will thrive. This is why adults need to influence the norms that are established and avoid being backed off by silent or abrasive adolescent insistence on social independence. When adults allow themselves to be dismissed from the early adolescent social world, they risk ignoring and dismissing what happens there. Of course, every time they miss or dismiss an act of social cruelty, they encourage that kind of mistreatment to be accepted and even adopted as the norm. To reduce the incidents of social cruelty during the middle school years, school staff on all levels need to make clear that social cruelty isn't just "how it is" at this age, but rather that it doesn't have to be like this and that there is a better way.

There is a cycle here for adults to beware. As I have suggested, the root of social cruelty during the middle school years is early adolescent insecurity. When social cruelty is allowed to become the ruling norm in peer relationships, that security is further reduced by interactions that become more desperate and harsh.

Years ago, I spent an hour as an observer in the worst classroom for social cruelty I have ever seen, where the emotional damage being done was calculated and severe, and it probably had long-lasting formative effects on the offenders and the injured. Taunts and jeers were flung across the room; students huddled and laughed at a lone object of their derision;

defamatory notes were passed; two larger boys (kings of the hill) swept books off the desks of several quiet students, one of whom looked truly enraged; and a group of lesser lights followed the lead of a dominant girl by all pushing by another girl as though she wasn't even there. There wasn't much energy for academic learning in this classroom. I had the feeling that for the first-year teacher who feebly struggled for order, this would be that person's last class. It was chaos, and the "inmates" set the rules. Because I was an observer, an outsider, I had no sway with the students involved, but I was able to report what I had witnessed to the principal who I am sure didn't want to hear what I had to say. I described early adolescent students tearing each other down in a classroom situation that would only do more damage, unless norms of social treatment were reset immediately. The cycle of social cruelty, I suggested, would become increasingly hard to reverse. Although an extreme case, this illustrates for me why adults at school need to take a stand against social cruelty and help create a safe school environment.

Because social cruelty is an ongoing problem embedded in the insecurities created by early adolescent change, it takes ongoing commitment by the school to combat it. A one shot program just won't solve the problem. From the outset of each school year and throughout the school year itself, norms for safe social treatment among students need to be specified, ratified, publicized, and supervised. Students need to be told what mean behaviors are off-limits and why, as well as what socially considerate behaviors are valued and why.

The message of school safety needs to come from the administration, supported by the counselors, and taught and discussed by teachers in the classroom. Initiative from adults in the school can raise the issue with students. When students know that the adults are aware of and are opposed to social cruelty behaviors, young people are encouraged to govern their conduct accordingly. Directly stated, adults in charge of the school want a safe place for students to learn, and this requires the following:

- No mean teasing

- No punitive exclusion

- No threatening bullying

- No slanderous rumoring

- No ganging up against anyone

With distracted early adolescent students, social cruelty only makes effective teaching that much harder to accomplish. Principals, teachers, and counselors all have significant roles to play in their respective spheres of influence with students.

- A principal can set the expected school-wide norm of student treatment by ruling out acts of social cruelty, setting sanctions for violations, and specifying norms of good citizenship to be followed. *A principal is in charge of setting and communicating school-wide policies about social cruelty.*

- A teacher can instruct and lead classroom discussions about social cruelty and help students create a code of social consideration for their treatment of each other. *A teacher is in charge of educating students about social cruelty.*

- A counselor can meet with individual offenders and injured parties involved in incidents of social cruelty in order to aid in recovery from harm, assuming responsibility for doing harm, and reconciling the relationship so harm does not occur again. *A counselor is in charge of intervening after cases of social cruelty occur.*

Let's start with the principal, because it is this person's authority and leadership that is the major bulwark against social cruelty. Leadership determines priorities, sets objectives, and provides support for meeting instructional and social objectives, such as academic learning and safe student treatment of each other. When a principal declares that creating a safe school is a high priority, backing up words he or she says with actions taken, then those below are most likely to fall in line.

What the Principal Can Do

The principal is the leader of the school. He or she has the power to set and communicate priorities, and that can include creating and maintaining a safe school. For students to be safe, they need to be able to answer "yes" to four questions:

- Does the principal know about the reality of social cruelty?

- Does the principal care about reducing the incidence of social cruelty?

- Does the principal circulate and talk to students about what's going on?

- Does the principal take actions and expect staff to take actions in order to prevent social cruelty where they can and intervene when they cannot?

In a safe school, students feel they can rely on a structure of social authority that is designed and implemented by sufficient adult supervision to keep them safe. The principal is the ruling authority in the school. When that authority is both visible and approachable for students, school can feel more secure.

He or she sets the expectations for the school, and that includes expectations for how students treat each other. The principal can declare to all the students that this will be a *safe* school. "Safe" means that no one will live in fear of or be the object of social treatment meant to hurt—teasing, exclusion, bullying, rumoring, or ganging up.

- In a safe school, students can enjoy each other's company and concentrate on learning.

- In a safe school, students are also encouraged to take citizen responsibility for reporting and speaking up about any unsafe activity that occurs.

- And in a safe school, there is adequate supervision by adults.

In general, the larger the school and the less familiar students are with each other, the harder it is for adults to adequately supervise so many students and the easier it is for acts of social cruelty to go unchecked. Freedom from adult supervision can allow freedom for social cruelty to occur.

Think of the less supervised locations in the school. These are the social congregating places before and after school, the school grounds and playground, the lunchroom or cafeteria, the hallways, the stairwells, the locker rooms, the bathrooms, down by the auditorium or gym, even the parking lot, and of course the bus. All are locations less adequately supervised than the classroom. While in the classroom, a seasoned teacher usually brings more supervisory attention to students than a new or a substitute teacher does. The less the adult presence, the greater the opportunity for acts of social cruelty to occur. Acts of social cruelty can be opportunistic. Wherever there is no adult presence, isolated individuals can more easily become victims. Sometimes community and parent volunteers can help increase the supervisory coverage in the school. It is important to adequately supervise school zones where an adult presence is not typically around.

In an increasing number of states, student safety is not just a school option; it is a legal obligation. Schools have a legal duty to protect the safety of students in their care, and that includes safety from mistreatment by each other. More than twenty states have now enacted anti-bullying and anti-harassment laws that apply to student behavior in the schools. *Ensuring student safety is the job of the school.*

The principal has the authority for rule making and recognition. He or she can shape the citizen behavior of students by rewarding acts of social consideration and sanctioning acts of social cruelty. At the outset of the year, the principal can declare to students what "safe school" *policies* constitute. The goal of these policies is to create a social climate in which students can enjoy each other's company and concentrate on learning. Social cruelty behaviors can be listed and described as actions that are prohibited in the school: the use of teasing, excluding, bullying, rumoring, or ganging up to deliberately hurt another student. The principal can also describe *procedures* for dealing with violations. For example, any student found engaging in these activities could be sent to the principal's office, where that student will be asked to call a parent. The student will explain the reason for the call and request that the parents come to school for a conference, at which time all involved will fully discuss the incident and explore the disciplinary options. The options available could include amends to the victim, service to the school, counseling about victim impact, detention, and suspension in repeated or severe cases.

There must be a specified adult contact in place to whom significant acts of social cruelty can be reported. The administrative message is "We want to know when significant or repeated mistreatment occurs, because what creates a lack of safety for one endangers the social safety of all. We want a school in which everyone feels safe to learn. We will not tolerate behavior that endangers or harms anyone."

"Zero tolerance," however, is not enough, because it only prohibits antisocial behavior and provides sanctions for infractions. The problem with punishment is that it has no instructional power. It responds to what should not have been done, but it doesn't prescribe any positive alternatives. In a family, it would be like punishing children for wrestling over who gets to play with a toy without ever teaching them strategies for sharing (such as using a timer for taking turns). In the same way, it is important that principals and teachers tell students that fighting is prohibited to curb violence at school. However, in a safe school, these authorities also provide mediation of disputes, as well as conflict resolution and mediation training for students to educate them in how to resolve differences in nonviolent ways.

If a school is going to have *zero tolerance* policies regarding social cruelty, they need *zero likelihood* policies as well. Zero tolerance is reactive—after the fact of mistreatment, it corrects the wrongdoers. Whereas zero likelihood is proactive—before the fact, it instructs about how to constructively treat each other. *Prohibition does not stop social cruelty; education does.* In fact, sometimes protection can do more harm than good.

As for school security measures, they are always problematic, because they are double-edged. They assure and frighten at the same time. Identity checks, metal detectors, surveillance cameras, emergency preparedness routines, lockdowns, all done in the name of safety, come at a price. Intended to provide physical safety, they each increase the sense of danger at school. In a truly safe school, such measures would be minimized, because students would have little to fear. The psychology of personal protection and social security is always self-defeating to some degree. For example, students who bring a concealed weapon to school for self-protection only arm themselves, against the danger that they fear and helps them keep in mind the frightening world in which they must survive.

This is not to say that schools should not take adequate security measures; only that such measures taken for physical safety often arouse some degree of psychological danger. It's like going through security screening at the airport. It reminds us of terrorist possibilities. Thus, safety drills in a school (such as practicing a lockdown in response to a threat of student violence) are not entirely reassuring to those participating in the exercise.

Because early adolescents are so needful of peer belonging, and thus so vulnerable to social cruelty, one of the most powerful ways to moderate this influence is by increasing the influence of adults. Ideally, one way a principal can accomplish this goal is by assigning every student an individual advisor among the faculty and staff at the school. The purpose of this is not to provide some kind of personal counseling but simply to create a *special interest relationship*. The adult has a special interest in getting to know the student who in turn has a special chance to get to know that adult. An advisor encourages constructive engagement and acts as a resource for the student. Most importantly, this adult responds to the mature and responsible aspect of the student at a time when peers tend to reinforce one's less mature and less responsible side. This adult can even become an advocate should any adjustment difficulties at school arise. In general, although not absolutely necessary, pairing boys with men and girls with women may work best because of the modeling influence a same-sex relationship provides.

Finally, the principal can encourage a parent-teacher partnership for school safety so that school and home keep each other adequately informed and work in tandem, watching for any trouble spots and supporting any intervention. Teachers and parents need to be on the same side of school safety. Now consider what a teacher might do to counteract social cruelty and help the cause of social safety in the classroom.

What the Teacher Can Do

From what I have seen, many middle school age students tend to believe the following about adults at school:

- They don't know much about the social cruelty going on.

- They don't much care about social cruelty going on.

- They can't do much about social cruelty going on.

The sense that the school staff is totally out of the loop discredits these adults in the eyes of students who feel they must shut up, gut up, and handle acts of social cruelty alone, or it convinces students that they can commit them with impunity. This sense of social independence isolates young people from adult assistance. This is why teachers must dispel all three beliefs on a classroom level. First, they have to demonstrate their knowledge of social cruelty— that it exists, what it is, how it works, and what it costs. Second, they have to declare why they do not want it going on—social cruelty is not emotionally safe; it is not ethically right; and it interferes with education. And third, they have to enlist students in creating and abiding by a program for reducing the incidents of social cruelty and promoting social consideration instead—empowering young people to construct and follow a code of social treatment that feels safe and supportive.

What follows are some instructional approaches a teacher can take when opening up the subject of social cruelty with students. At least three topics need to be discussed: *early adolescence, peer relationships,* and *social meanness.*

Introducing Early Adolescence

As an outside instructor working with students, the best way I have found to open a classroom discussion about social cruelty with middle school age students is by starting with a discussion of early adolescent change. So I explain how *none of them are children anymore.* Now they are all adolescents, starting a process of development that will graduate them into independence and young adulthood ten to twelve years hence.

Starting between the ages of nine and thirteen, they begin changing. What they noticed was a growing dissatisfaction with being defined and treated as "just a child" anymore. In place of being content with one's traditional interests, with one's comfortable place in the family circle, and with the company of old childhood friends, now there is a desire for more worldly freedom, acting older and finding different companions.

Wanting more freedom at home and out in the world, tensions and disagreements with parents usually increase. Parents hold on when young people wish they would let go, or at least ease up. By pushing against and pulling away from parents, the young person starts a process of growing apart from them that will finally come to an end when he or she claims responsible adulthood in the early- to mid-twenties.

Having given this kind of a general introduction, a teacher can stop describing the change from childhood into adolescence and can start asking the students to continue it themselves. One useful way to generate ideas for this discussion of how they have in fact become different from the child they used to be is by asking them to fill out a *comparison chart*.

AS ADOLESCENTS:

We are_____

We do _____

We like _____

We have_____

We know _____

We look_____

We need_____

We worry about_____

We wish for_____

We get down about _____

We get excited for_____

We care about _____

AS CHILDREN:

We were _____

We did _____

We liked_____

We had_____

We knew_____

We looked_____

We needed_____

We worried about _____

We wished for_____

We got down about _____

We got excited for _____

We cared about_____

Next the teacher can have the students discuss the changes they have seen in themselves as they separated from their childhood.

Then the class can talk about what the hardest changes are and why, as well as what managing so much change feels like.

Introducing Peer Relationships

Next the teacher can move into the complexities of peer relationships at this changing age. This is a time for more social independence, and that includes the construction of a separate social community of peers.

These young friends and acquaintances now become a competing social influence with one's family at home. These are the peers who provide essential companionship on the journey to young manhood and young womanhood. They become among the most powerfully bonded and influential relationships in one's life, because it is with them that one shares the trials, challenges, and adventures of growing up.

These relationships with peers, however, particularly during the middle school years, are not easy because everyone is changing. Most people are deviled with feelings of insecurity. No longer a child but not yet an adult, how are they supposed to define and conduct themselves? No longer a little boy or little girl, how are they supposed to conduct themselves as young men or young women? Beginning adolescence feels awkward, because it is the age of in-between. Young people can feel insecure for many reasons. There is fitting in less comfortably at home. There is boredom, because they may not know what do with themselves now.

There is self-consciousness, as bodily changes one does not control and may not like occur. And there is the constant struggle to keep up with and stay connected in a social world of peers who are all changing as fast as they are.

Now it is easier to feel hurt and to be hurt by others. It is also easier to hurt others when feeling hurt or preventing getting hurt in the future. At a time when having friends and belonging to a community of friends becomes more important, maintaining friendships also becomes harder to do. There is much more push and shove now as everyone competes for a secure social place during a more insecure time. Now the teacher can give each student a list of common social hardships and ask them to check any they have either experienced themselves or seen firsthand.

HARDSHIPS IN GETTING ALONG

_____ *People wanting to be your friend just because you're popular.*

_____ *Gossiping about people.*

_____ *People telling lies about other people.*

_____ *Losing a good friend who makes new friends who won't include you.*

_____ *Being teased.*

_____ *Being laughed at.*

_____ *Spreading rumors to attack someone's reputation.*

_____ *People ganging up on you.*

_____ *Ganging up on someone else.*

_____ *Making fun of someone behind his or her back.*

_____ *Having a good friend turn against you.*

_____ *Being told no one wants you as a friend.*

_____ *Quarreling with a good friend over your new friends.*

_____ *Having a friend tell others about a secret you confided.*

_____ *Feeling jealous when a good friend wants to be with someone else.*

_____ *Seeing a friend change into a different person.*

_____ *Competing against friends for boys.*

_____ *Competing against friends for girls.*

_____ *Bullying other people.*

_____ *Having a friend pass you over for other friends.*

_____ *Taking or defacing another person's belongings.*

_____ *People making fun of your appearance.*

_____ *Having your locker vandalized.*

_____ *Being kicked out of a group.*

_____ *Receiving prank calls that hurt your feelings.*

_____ *Receiving emails, text messages, or instant messages that attack you.*

_____ *Feeling like you have to follow the lead of a dominating friend.*

_____ *Someone threatening "to get" you.*

_____ *Forced to give over something or get hurt.*

_____ *Being given the silent treatment.*

_____ *Acting fake to get along.*

_____ *People pressuring you to do what you're not supposed to do.*

_____ *Hurting people through nicknames.*

_____ *Fighting to prove how tough you are.*

_____ *Worrying about not being safe at school.*

_____ *People cutting each other down with insults.*

_____ *Being left out of a party when your friends were invited.*

_____ *Going to a party when you feel shy and not outgoing.*

_____ *Pretending to have a good time when you're not.*

_____ *Writing notes about one person to another person.*

_____ *Breaking up someone else's friendship.*

_____ *Organizing a whispering campaign.*

_____ *Keeping others on the outside of a group.*

_____ *Pressuring people to go along if they want to be included.*

_____ *Losing a best friend.*

_____ *Wishing you had as much as some other people.*

_____ *Being spoken to one day and ignored the next.*

_____ *Going along with the group even though it feels wrong.*

_____ *Someone who won't talk to you in class but can be friendly outside school.*

_____ *Giving up a friend to get socially ahead.*

_____ *Having a friend stop talking to you.*

_____ *Having friends who don't stand up for you.*

_____ *Not standing up for a friend.*

_____ *Being dishonest with people to get on their good side.*

_____ *Envying people more popular than yourself.*

_____ *Not having the right thing to wear.*

_____ *Feeling trapped by a best friend who is too possessive.*

_____ *Acting like you don't care when you really do.*

_____ *Being treated like you're not looking or acting cool.*

_____ *Being put down for not keeping up with fashion or what is latest.*

Now the teacher can ask students to add any other hardships in getting along that are not on the list, and then ask them to check the five hardships they believe are the worst, being mindful of the reasons why. Finally, the class can form discussion groups of four students, with each group coming up with a consensus agreement of the five worst hardships.

The list of social difficulty and social cruelty behaviors brings the topic out in the open. Examining those behaviors, they access their experience. Talking among each other about these behaviors normalizes them for discussion. Coming to consensus over the "worst" hardships allows them to clarify and discuss which behaviors they agree are the worst and why. By picking out the worst, they identify behaviors with damage done, thereby laying the groundwork for a class discussion of the five major social cruelty behaviors: teasing, exclusion, bullying, rumoring, and ganging up. The teacher can point out that engaging in these behaviors is a *matter of choice*. People can *choose* to treat each other this way or not. When they do choose to treat each other badly, a lot of damage can be done.

Introducing Social Meanness

A teacher can explain how there are five basic kinds of social cruelty that are all aggressive and hostile in intent. That is, each one is intended to "get" somebody in the following ways:

• To hurt him or her

• To hurt him or her back

• To keep him or her from hurting the young person engaging in social cruelty

People act this way to feel better by making someone else feel worse. The problem is, if making someone feel worse is the best way people have of feeling better, then they are not feeling very good themselves. People who are not feeling hurt themselves have very little interest in hurting other people.

Then teachers can briefly teach the students about each of the five basic kinds of social cruelty—teasing, exclusion, bullying, rumoring, and ganging up. They should allow time for students to give examples of that kind of behavior (without naming names) after describing each, and discuss why people want to do it, what it feels like to be the victim of it, and how best to respond should it happen to them.

A teacher should never underestimate the power of discussion. It gets students to examine what they *think* about social cruelty.

And next time an inclination or opportunity arises, those thoughts—clarified in discussion—may cause the young person to refrain from participating in the future. So what content can a teacher share about each of the five kinds of social cruelty to lay the groundwork for a class discussion? Here are some short descriptions to get started.

What a Teacher Can Explain about Teasing

Teasing is the use of words to pick on or make fun of some aspect of another person about which he or she feels self-conscious, vulnerable, or insecure, putting him or her down in the teaser's eyes, the eyes of witnesses, and often in his or her own. The teaser seeks to contrast him or herself to something inferior or unattractive about the person teased. The payoff for the teaser is a feeling of superiority based on the comparison being made. Teasing can pick on someone based on his or her self-consciousness about appearance, vulnerability about incapacity, or insecurity from a lack of confidence.

Teasing is intended to humiliate with insults. Teasing preys on the *fear of being inferior.* "Something is wrong with me!" It undermines self-esteem. Someone can become a victim of *teasing* when given an insulting nickname, put down for reason of appearance or performance, ridiculed for standing out or not fitting in, or laughed at for what one says or doesn't know. *Teasing is the act of making fun of a difference in someone to criticize his or her person, diminish his or her social standing, and set him or her socially apart.* The cruel message is "There's something wrong with you." For the victim, it can increase self-criticism and lower self-worth.

What a Teacher Can Explain about Exclusion

Exclusion is the act of rejecting someone who wants a relationship with the excluder, denying him or her membership in a group, or subjecting him or her to social shunning. *Exclusion* is intended to isolate with rejection. By rejecting someone who wants a relationship, the excluder succeeds in making the other person feel inadequate. By denying someone membership who wants to join, the excluders succeed in making the person feel unpopular. "We don't have any more room at our lunch table, so sit somewhere else." By shunning someone who wants acknowledgment or recognition, the excluders succeed in making the other person feel isolated and alone.

In these cases, the excluder seeks to disassociate from, cut out, or totally ignore another person. The payoff for the excluder is the power to be socially selective, keep social competition down, and punish someone by outcasting him or her.

Someone can be a victim of *exclusion* when students ignore the person in class, deny the person a place at the table at lunch, see the person is not included in gatherings outside of school, shun classroom contact with the person so he or she feels isolated, or expel the person from membership in their group. *Exclusion is the act of refusing to let someone associate with others or join a group.* The cruel message is "You don't belong." Exclusion preys on the *fear of isolation.* "I will have no friends." For the victim, it can accentuate loneliness by limiting association or denying belonging.

What a Teacher Can Explain about Bullying

Bullying is the use of hostile actions or words to intimidate, coerce, or injure someone who is usually weaker or more vulnerable than the bully. *Bullying* is intended to intimidate with immanent or actual harm. By *intimidating*, the bully succeeds in making the other person feel threatened and afraid. By *coercing*, the bully succeeds in making the other person surrender something that the bully wants. By *hurting*, the bully succeeds in making the other person feel pain. In these cases, the bully seeks to menace, get his or her way with, or to hurt another person. The payoff for the bully is achieving a sense of supremacy. Bullies bully those who are weaker to feel strong.

Someone can be a victim of *bullying* when possessions are stolen or vandalized, when threats are made "to get you after school," when one is verbally attacked over the Internet or phone, or when the child is routinely hit or shoved or beaten up. *Bullying is the act of verbally or physically intimidating, injuring, coercing, or dominating another person.* The cruel message is "You can be pushed around." Bullying preys on the *fear of weakness.* "I won't be able to stand up for myself." For the victim, it can create a sense of impotence and even shame.

What a Teacher Can Explain about Rumoring

Rumoring is the creation and spreading of defamatory information about someone that is usually partly or totally false in order to slander that person's reputation and reduce his or her social standing. *Rumoring* is intended to slander with confidential truths or blatant lies. Gossip is what spreads the hearsay of rumor around. Rumor questions someone's behavior or motivation, describes someone in negative ways, accuses someone of supposed wrongdoing, reveals supposed secret information about someone, warns about the supposed dangers of someone, fabricates a story to break up a relationship, or starts a feud or fight between people.

The power of rumor is that it is negative, difficult to source, hard to verify, quickly spread, increasingly exaggerated with each retelling, and legitimized with repetition. It plays on people's ignorance, fears, jealousies, longings, prejudices, grievances, resentments, and dreams, and it is used to advance their personal agendas. At worst, rumor inflicts character assassination. It becomes accepted as common knowledge about someone, damaging how that person is publicly known.

Someone can be a victim of *rumors* when others circulate salacious notes, make up and tell malicious stories (in person, over the phone, or via the Internet) about a person to create a false impression that he or she will have trouble living down, or confide secrets trustingly told to now be used against the confider. *Rumoring is the act of using gossip to spread lies or secrets about another person that demeans his or her social reputation.* The cruel message is "You can't control the bad that people say about you that others are ready to believe." Rumor preys on the *fear of defamation.* "People will say mean things about me." For the victim, it can show how no one can control his or her reputation.

What a Teacher Can Explain about Ganging Up

Ganging up is getting other people to take one's side against someone else. It is also when a group aggresses against an individual using any (or any combination of) the other four kinds of social cruelty—teasing, exclusion, bullying, rumoring—to demean, ostracize, injure, or defame the person. *Ganging up* is intended to pit the group against an individual. Because the social cruelty is no longer one-on-one but many-against-one, the effects are greatly amplified. To the victim, it can become overwhelming. Ganging up makes teasing more scornful, exclusion more isolating, bullying more threatening, and rumoring more slanderous. Ganging up is a very serious numbers game calculated to communicate mass dislike, create a common object of ridicule, conspire to blame someone, demonstrate greater power, or build group solidarity.

Those ganging up feel more powerful from being part of a concerted social action. The person ganged up on feels more helpless, because so many people have united against him or her. Someone can be a victim of being *ganged up* on when multiple students verbally or physically use any of the other four kinds of social cruelty to attack a single person. It creates a sense of solidarity in the attackers and extreme vulnerability in the object of their attack. *Ganging up is the act of the many using their greater number to all torment the one.* The cruel message is "You have no friends to support you, only enemies against you." Ganging up preys on the *fear of persecution.* "Everyone will turn against me." For the victim, it can fulfill the fear of being downtrodden and outcast.

After introducing each of the five kinds of social cruelty, teachers should ask students to discuss what it's like both to give and receive each tactic. To accomplish this task, the teacher can divide the class in two, one half determining five motivations and benefits for participating in that social cruelty, the other half determining five impacts and costs of being the target of that kind of social cruelty. The power of discussion is that it focuses attention, raises awareness, develops understanding, and influences future choice. It makes students self-conscious about their behavior and how they will treat each other in the future. Now the teacher has established the groundwork for students to consider the larger social lessons that social cruelty can teach and the power of social treatment in relationships.

Teaching the Larger Social Lessons

Teachers can turn the varieties of social cruelty to extremely powerful instructional effect. They should start by leading a discussion that seeks to relate the five forms of social cruelty to the larger social-psychological issues they present:

- A discussion of teasing can inform students about the harm of *social labeling*. Name calling can reduce a complex individual to a single negative identifier. For example, call someone nothing but "worthless," and one may feel that term encompasses most of how that person acts and thinks. In this way, social labeling can lead to *prejudice*, which at worst can take advantage of the bad name to justify mistreating the person named. Discussion question: In the larger society, how do people label other people in prejudicial ways, and how does it feel to be so labeled?

- A discussion of exclusion can inform students about the harm of *social selection*. Keeping others out can also reduce people's freedom to participate. For example, deny someone from joining a group, and they are denied what group membership allows others to enjoy and achieve. Social selection can lead to *discrimination*. Discussion question: In the larger society, how do people exclude others in discriminatory ways, and how does it feel to be left out and kept out?

- A discussion of bullying can inform students about the harm of *social harassment*. For example, being subjected to continual threats and coercion, one can become intimidated. Social harassment can lead to *oppression*. Discussion question: In the larger society, how do people subordinate others in threatening ways, and how does it feel to be so oppressed?

- A discussion of rumor can inform students about the harm of *social hearsay*. For example, by passing on unverified accusations, someone can shape public opinion with malicious lies. Social hearsay can become the means for public *slander*. Discussion question: In the larger society, how do people defame others, and how does it feel to have one's reputation attacked this way?

- A discussion of ganging up can inform students about the damage of *social obedience*. For example, carried along by the will of the group, or afraid to oppose it, members can participate in acts of harm they would never do individually. Social obedience can support *persecution*. Discussion question: In the larger society, how do people get caught up in following along with group sentiment and action, and how does it feel to collaborate in doing harm?

What this instruction can make clear is that while social cruelty is a part of their middle school experience, the tactics used are part of more widespread societal behavior. In this sense, middle school is just a microcosm of society. If students can be taught to see this connection, they may become more sensitive to the social and psychological issues at play in the larger world. Then there is an opportunity for students to learn some lessons about social treatment.

Teaching about Social Treatment

Social treatment involves how young people choose to act and react to each other and the effects such actions and reactions have on the relationship. Because social cruelty is a form of social treatment, teachers can then explain the *six consequences of social treatment* to their students:

- *How you treat other people is how you establish your social reputation.* Treat people kindly, and you are likely to be known as kind; treat them meanly, and you are likely to be known as mean. How you act toward others is how people come to see you.

- *How you treat other people is how you treat yourself.* Treat other people kindly, and you treat yourself as a kind person; treat them meanly, and you treat yourself as a mean person. How you act toward others creates the image of yourself.

- *How you treat other people is how you encourage them to treat you.* Treat other people kindly, and they are likely to treat you kindly in return; treat them meanly, and they are likely to treat you meanly back. How you act toward others affects how others act to you.

- *How you treat others each time forms a habit of how you treat people most of the time.* The more often you are nice or mean to people, the more you get accustomed to treating others nicely or meanly. How you act toward others shapes how you become.

- *How you treat other people shapes how they see themselves.* Treat another person kindly, and he or she feels worthy of consideration; treat that person meanly, and he or she may feel undeserving of being treated well. How you act toward others affects how they perceive themselves.

- *How you treat other people contributes to the social climate in which you live.* Each time you treat another person kindly or meanly, you influence everyone's feeling about the community. How you act toward others contributes to how everyone treats each other.

Social treatment is a matter of personal choice. Depending on the treatment choices students make, that decides the climate of the independent social world they are creating. By creating a code of social treatment, they can specify the quality of interaction with each other they would like to have. A teacher can help students develop such a classroom code.

Creating a Code of Social Treatment

When starting a class discussion about how to build a code of ethical treatment of each other, the *rule of reciprocity* is a serviceable place to start. It is based on that "golden rule" that is found, in one form or another, in many faiths around the world, among many different periods of human history. Essentially it recommends "Treat others as you want them to treat you." This has both *empathetic* and *ethical* parts. Empathetically, it advises acting based on how one would feel to be on the receiving end of that action. Ethically, it advises consulting one's beliefs about what constitutes morally "right" conduct.

A teacher can work within his or her immediate sphere of influence to help students construct *a classroom code of social consideration*. Involving students in this exercise is important, because they are most likely to support principles of treating each other that they helped create.

One effective way of starting is for the teacher to take his or her own conduct as a starting place. "Tell me how you would like me to treat you for you to feel good about yourself and our relationship." And among the *qualities* the students usually come up with are "respect" and "fairness" and "consideration." Then the teacher needs to specify the meaning of these general terms by translating them into actions or *behaviors*. "What would I do or not do to demonstrate the qualities you value?" In order to show respect, listen to all of what a student has to say. To show fairness, the behavior might be calling on everyone, not just a favored few. And to show consideration, don't criticize a student for not knowing the answer to a question or giving a wrong answer. Next the teacher should brainstorm the qualities and behaviors students would like to characterize their treatment of each other.

In constructing a code, help students develop their sense of community. For example, ask students which kind of community would they like school to be?

COMMUNITY X	OR	COMMUNITY Y
School feels:		
Safe	or	Threatening?
Kind	or	Mean?
Positive	or	Negative?
Tolerant	or	Intolerant?
Friendly	or	Unfriendly?
Caring	or	Hostile?
Helpful	or	Hurtful?
Trusting	or	Suspicious?
Relaxing	or	Stressful?
Cooperative	or	Combative?
Connected	or	Lonely?

What kind of school community do students want to live in? By their individual treatment of each other, they create the community of peer relationships in the school. They also influence those relationships by how they respond to acts of social cruelty that they witness happening to others. This is the hard issue of social responsibility. To what degree do they want to get involved by reporting or intervening when acts of social cruelty occur to others?

Standing Up for Someone

Always worth discussing with students is what they feel they would or should do if they see some friend (or even someone they may not know) being mistreated by another student or students at school. At an insecure age when it is already hard to stand up for themselves, it can take twice as much bravery and confidence on their account to stand up for someone else. To do or say nothing, however, means they are supporting what they witness with their inaction. There are a series of questions a teacher can raise for this discussion:

- *When should you stand up for someone else?* This is a question of *citizen responsibility.* Part of the answer might involve when you have the courage to become involved in what is not directly happening to you. Another part of the answer might involve when you think your involvement could make a difference.

- *How do you know a situation is right for your involvement?* This is a question of *ethical responsibility.* Part of the answer might be because you wouldn't want to be mistreated that way. Another part of the answer might be because you want to interfere in something that is wrong.

- *When should you get an adult authority involved?* This is the question of *reporting responsibility.* Part of the answer might be because you lack sufficient power to make a difference by yourself. Another part of the answer might be because you think the school should take a stand against this kind of behavior.

- *When should you leave the object of mistreatment alone to fend for him or herself?* This is the question of *respecting responsibility*. Part of the answer might be when the person is doing nothing to speak up or stand up for his or herself. Another part of the answer might include finding a way to deal with the situation that makes them stronger.

Additional questions to get students to discuss might include the following:

- Have you ever stood up for someone, and how did it feel when you did?

- Has anyone ever stood up for you, and how did that feel then?

- Has a friend ever failed to stand up for you, and how did that feel?

- Have you ever failed to stand up for a friend, and how did that feel?

The teacher can also give an example, mentioned earlier in this book, of a graceful rescue by a popular eighth-grade girl who saw a sixth grader in the hall being teased or threatened to the point of tears by three older girls. Without saying a word to the four girls, the rescuer entered the gathering, took the sixth grader by the hand, said "let's go," and led her away.

There were four aspects to the power of this intervention. First, without being told a word (actually being pointedly ignored), the three girls knew that a popular (and socially powerful) girl disapproved of their actions. Second, the three girls knew—from the clasped hand connected between the two—that to continue to mess with the sixth grader meant that they would be dealing with the popular girl hereafter. Third, the social reputation of the sixth grader now included being well connected to a popular girl. And fourth, popularity had taken a stand against social cruelty. This last point is worth the teacher remembering. To encourage a reduction in social cruelty in a school, it really helps to enlist popular students. This way, popularity becomes allied with bringing the best out in people, as opposed to social cruelty that brings out the worst. When prominent students in positions of social influence take stands against acts of social cruelty, it makes those actions less desirable and more costly.

A teacher can also preempt social cruelty from happening in the class. She can declare that the classroom is hers to run. This means the teacher has rules for how people communicate with each other and how they treat each other when under her instruction. For example, there must be no name calling of the teasing kind. There must be no exclusion and isolating of anyone. There must be no bullying and pushing anyone around. There must be no spreading rumors by whispering campaigns or passing notes about each other. And there must be no ganging up by lots of people laughing when someone gives a wrong answer or makes a mistake.

It is important for the teacher to acknowledge that the rules of classroom treatment and communication she insists on may be very different from those that students are used to following with friends outside of school and within their families, and that is okay. "If my rules of social treatment are different from those in your life outside of school, that does not mean I am in disagreement with or critical of how you behave away from here. It only means that while you are here, you are expected to follow my rules."

One of the most powerful things a teacher can do is to create an *inclusive classroom* that is tolerant of diversity, but this will not happen if she leaves the matter of where students sit and how students congregate up to the young people themselves. Left to decide, students will choose to sit by friends and congregate in cliques. Familiarity, similarity, and popularity will rule. In this situation, it can become common for a student to go unselected when other students are picking out work groups, excluded because of being different or unpopular.

Teachers cannot only assign seating, but they can take charge of the formation of work groups—and they should. This is always a responsibility worth holding. Their goal is to keep physically and socially mixing people. By proximity of seating and work partnerships, they want them to get to know other students who would otherwise be avoided or ignored. When the teacher does the social seating and the group assignments, no one is left out, and everyone is socially exposed to everyone else, getting to know and getting along with each other. And no one can be faulted for whom he or she is associating with because the teacher set up those associations. The jock feels okay about being in a study group with a computer geek, because the teacher arranged that group assignment (and he may discover that the computer geek is not so weird after all, just as the computer geek may discover that the jock is not so dumb).

Finally, teachers can instruct others about social cruelty by having students read and discuss an extremely relevant literary text. The great allegory of *social cruelty among abandoned youth groups* is William Golding's *Lord of the Flies*, a book that resonates with many early adolescents not simply because it is short and mostly written in dialogue, but because they recognize how it is socially true. Following the survival instincts of their early adolescent age, the shipwrecked young people in the story form a society without any adult guidance, supervision, or intervention, one in which they become increasingly destructive toward each other. Fittingly, the social cruelty stops with the reentry of an adult authority at the end of the book. Until then, young people become victims of their insecurity, vulnerability, and independence, abusing power as they grow. Students can discuss which character they most identify with, and they can discuss why they think these young people ended up treating each other as they did.

Sometimes schools are their own enemy when it comes to creating student intolerance of diversity. Schools that academically track and stratify students based on performance risk creating social separations between accelerated and low performing students who have no classroom contact with each other, because academic placement keeps them apart. At worst, it creates school within a school (such as a magnet school within a regular school), some students receiving enriched content or advanced instruction that those lower performing student groups are denied. Now intergroup tensions can result, and acts of social cruelty may occur, because groups of students are academically segregated from each other and a sense of common community is not shared.

What the Counselor Can Do

While the administrator can treat social cruelty as a violation of school safety and the teacher can make social cruelty a focus of discussion, the counselor can deal with social cruelty as a case of personal and interpersonal damage that needs restorative attention.

Because social cruelty like bullying violates the rules of school safety, these acts are an administrative matter. Hearings and sanctions need to take place. Because these acts impact individual well-being and student relationships, they are also a counseling matter. For the counselor, more important than assigning blame and deciding punishment is ministering to the emotional damage and repairing the injured relationships.

An angry twelve-year-old boy is on a bullying tear, picking

on victims wherever he can find them, causing unhappiness, and no one knows why until, after the fact, the counselor discovers that he himself is feeling victim of a sudden and unexpected parental divorce. In counseling, the job entails helping him learn how to deal with hurt feelings without hurting others, without resorting to social cruelty to cope with the injury he has received. There is also victim impact counseling to explore. The offender needs help making an empathetic connection to the ones he has harmed. Those harmed need support to talk out their hurt feelings. And (if all parties are willing) a meeting where the offender and the harmed can better understand each other and develop a more constructive way of getting along together needs to occur. The counselor can help facilitate the discussion of the actions that took place, the harm that was done, and the reparation that might be made.

The counselor's role is a complicated one, predicated on three principles:

- When any individual is significantly harmed by social cruelty, a need for emotional recovery from that harm is created.

- When any individual does harm by committing social cruelty, an obligation on behalf of the harmed to right the harm is created.

- When a student relationship has been damaged by social cruelty, social reconciliation of that relationship needs to occur.

Then there are those relationships where students become stuck being mean to each other—for example, rivalries in which boys resort to mean teasing and taking shots at each other or in which girls resort to rumoring and spreading lies about each other. In each case, even the best students only know to treat each other badly. Gathering together each group to talk about what is going on, the counselor can provide other options for managing tensions and grievances and conflicts, teaching problem solving skills that preserve safe boundaries for all concerned. Two groups of students who are bent on getting back at each other are helped to find ways to cooperate with each other.

In Conclusion

During the middle school years, it takes the united efforts of principal, teachers, and counselors, not to mention the active involvement of parents, to keep incidents of social cruelty among early adolescents under control. To moderate social cruelty, school staff must make an ongoing effort to help early adolescents avoid becoming their own worst enemies by creating a community with each other that feels socially unsafe. This effort must be clear, constant, and consistent, because the developmental insecurity of early adolescence, and the heightened risk that social independence will degenerate into social cruelty is not going to simply disappear.

The principal needs to specify a norm for social treatment that rules out acts of social cruelty and applies sanctions should violations occur. Teachers need to instruct and discuss social cruelty with students, and create a code of social consideration that will be followed in each classroom community. In incidents of social cruelty, counselors need to work with offenders and injured parties to help sensitize the offender, to help the injured party recover, to make restoration for harm, and to reconcile relationships so that harm is not done again. And parent involvement needs to be enlisted in order to monitor any involvement in, effects of, or information about acts of social cruelty that may come home.

It costs school staff significant effort to counteract social cruelty, but it is far more costly if they do not. Lack of social safety from acts of social cruelty will reduce academic focus, and some young people will be encouraged to develop habits of social mistreatment that will only become more destructive in the high school years ahead.

As young people, in the name of social independence, want the adult world to back off and allow them to manage their own business with each other at this period of growth, salient adults—parents at home and staff at school—must insist on staying involved. Youth groups that are abandoned by adults during the middle school years are at the highest risk of social cruelty. The role of adults is to positively influence the social development of early adolescents during this formative time.

THE GIFTS OF ADVERSITY: GOOD LESSONS FROM BAD TREATMENT

What was middle school like?" I asked the student who was just finishing his first year of high school.

He laughed and shook his head. "What a mess! I learned a lot in middle school that got me ready for high school. Not so much from the teachers. More from what other students taught. I learned to take care of myself. I toughened up."

"How so?" I asked.

"In middle school there were some hard times. I guess there are for everyone. I got called names. I got pushed around. I got left out. I got a lot of stuff that wasn't fun. Sixth grade was pretty edgy, but by eighth grade, I knew how to take the bad and stand up for myself. Dealing with middle school gave me the confidence to make it in high school."

"Any single piece of advice you'd pass along to kids starting middle school now?"

Then, like a seasoned veteran, this is what he immediately said: "Don't act scared."

I would never wish social cruelty on anyone. However, if it comes your children's way, remember that by helping them grow stronger, some powerful lessons can be learned. There are true gifts from facing this adversity that a young person can claim:

- "From being *teased*, I learned that the insults and put-downs are about people wanting to be mean, not about anything wrong with me."

- "From being *excluded*, I learned to enjoy my own company and to make new friends, not hang out with people who didn't want to be with me."

- "From being *bullied*, I learned to respect myself for having what it took to face what I didn't like each day, sometimes feared, but was strong enough to endure."

- "From being *rumored*, I learned that I can't control the lies people say about me or what others may believe, but I can always know the truth about myself."

- "From being *ganged up on*, I learned that no matter how lonely it can feel to have many people against me, there are other people, like my parents, who love me and are always on my side."

Social cruelty can make school a daunting place. Therefore, for the young person who has been targeted for social cruelty, it is an act of bravery to go to school each day. Much more is now at stake than formal classroom education because the young person is tested by a greater challenge—fear. While few experiences erode self-esteem as badly as giving into fear, nothing builds self-esteem as powerfully as gathering the courage to face fear down.

I wrote this book to empower parents to in turn empower their sons or daughters to face the social cruelties of middle school. By treating these unwelcome experiences as a challenge from which to grow, the adolescent can become stronger, just as parental support in these unhappy situations can help create a stronger family. To do this, I believe parents must first be sensitive to the insecurities of the early adolescent age. Second, they must be aware of the complexities that young people encounter when creating a socially independent world of peers. And third, they must be knowledgeable about the common forms that social cruelty takes—teasing, exclusion, bullying, rumoring, and ganging up.

To support their young person who is now living in a world where social cruelty is more common and usually more vicious, parents must be knowledgeable, empathetic, and supportive at an awkward time when adolescence is causing them and their young teenager to start growing apart. Despite the early adolescent's push away from parents to become more socially independent, the young person needs parental counsel to deal with his or her newfound social independence with peers.

This is no time to abandon your teenagers just because they want to be left alone to manage their own lives. The parental goals are to stay sufficiently involved in their early adolescent's life at middle school to help ensure social safety, to encourage strong self-esteem, to support solid friendships, and to supervise academic performance in preparation for the high school years.

RECOMMENDED READING

For those interested in learning more about early adolescence and social cruelty, there are a number of helpful books available.

About Early Adolescence

Pickhardt, Carl. *Stop the Screaming: How to Turn Angry Conflict with Your Child into Positive Communication*. New York: Palgrave Macmillan, 2009.

Pickhardt, Carl. *The Connected Father: Understanding Your Unique Role and Responsibilities during Your Child's Adolescence*. New York: Palgrave Macmillan, 2007.

Pipher, Mary. *Reviving Ophelia: Saving the Selves of Adolescent Girls*. New York: Ballantine Books, 1994.

Pollack, William. *Real Boys: Rescuing Our Sons from the Myths of Boyhood.* New York: Random House, 1998.

About Social Cruelty

Amstutz, Loraine Stutzman. *The Little Book of Restorative Discipline for Schools: Teaching Responsibility, Creating Caring Climates.* Intercourse, PA: Good Books, 2005.

Brown, Lyn Mikel. *Girlfighting: Betrayal and Rejection among Girls.* New York: New York University Press, 2005.

Coloroso, Barbara. *The Bully, the Bullied, and the Bystander: From Preschool to High School, How Parents and Teachers Can Help Break the Cycle of Violence.* New York: HarperResource, 2003.

Freedman, Judy S. *Easing the Teasing: Helping Your Child Cope with Name Calling, Ridicule, and Verbal Bullying.* Chicago: Contemporary Books, 2002.

Garbarino, James, and Ellen deLara. *And Words Can Hurt Forever: How to Protect Adolescents from Bullying, Harassment, and Emotional Violence.* New York: Free Press, 2003.

Golding, William. *Lord of the Flies.* New York: Penguin Books, 1999.

Karres, Erika V. Shearin. *Mean Chicks, Cliques, and Dirty Tricks: A Real Girl's Guide to Getting through the Day with Smarts and Style.* Avon, MA: Adams Media, 2004.

Kaufman, Gershen, Lev Raphael, and Pamela Espeland. *Stick Up for Yourself! Every Kid's Guide to Personal Power and Positive Self-Esteem.* Minneapolis: Free Spirit Publishing, 1999.

Kowalski, Robin M., Susan P. Limber, and Patricia W. Agatston. *Cyber Bullying.* Malden, MA: Blackwell Publishing, 2008.

Olweus, Dan. *Bullying at School.* Malden, MA: Blackwell Publishing, 1993.

Schoonover, Brian. *Zero Tolerance Discipline Policies.* Bloomington, IN: iUniverse, 2009.

Sommins, Rachel. *Odd Girl Out: The Hidden Culture of Aggression in Girls.* New York: Harcourt, 2002.

Swearer, Susan M., Dorothy L. Espelage, and Scott A. Napolitano. *Bullying, Prevention, and Intervention: Realistic Strategies for Schools.* New York: Guilford Publications, Inc., 2009.

Willard, Nancy E. *Cyberbullying and Cyberthreats: Responding to the Challenges of Online Social Aggression, Threats, and Distress.* Champaign, IL: Research Press, 2007.

Wiseman, Rosalind. *Queen Bees and Wannabes: Helping Your Daughter Survive Cliques, Gossip, Boyfriends, and Other Realities of Adolescence.* London: Piatkus, 2002.

Zehr, Howard. *The Little Book of Restorative Justice.* Intercourse, PA: Good Books, 2002.

ABOUT THE AUTHOR

Carl E. Pickhardt, PhD, is an author and psychologist in a private counseling and lecturing practice. He received his BA and MEd from Harvard, and earned his PhD from the University of Texas in Austin. He is a member of the American and Texas psychological associations. Dr. Pickhardt's books include *Stop the Screaming* (about family conflict), *The Future of Your Only Child* (about growing up as an only), *The Connected Father* (about adolescence), and many other parenting books. He writes a weekly parenting blog for Psychology Today about adolescence, "Surviving (your child's) Adolescence." See www.psychologytoday.com. He is married, with four grown children and one grandchild, and lives in Austin, Texas. For more information, see his website: www.carlpickhardt.com.

INDEX